EX LIBRIS

PRINTED IN ITALY

BOOK OF
JAMS, JELLIES AND CHUTNEYS

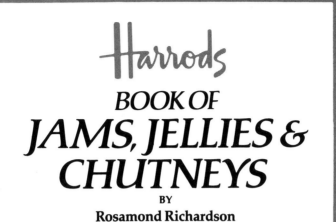

Harrods

BOOK OF
JAMS, JELLIES &
CHUTNEYS

BY
Rosamond Richardson

**ARBOR
HOUSE**

NEW YORK

First Impression 1987

Published in the United States of America by
Arbor House Publishing Company
and in Canada by Fitzhenry & Whiteside Ltd
by arrangement with Ebury Press, London

————————◆•◆•◆————————

EDITORS: Fiona MacIntyre, Barbara Croxford, Susan Friedland
ART DIRECTOR: Frank Phillips
DESIGNER: Marshall Art
PHOTOGRAPHY: Grant Symon
STYLIST: Sue Russell
HOME ECONOMISTS: Susanna Tee, Janet Smith and Maxine Clark

Ebury Press would like to thank Harrods, and their archivist
Margaret Baber, for allowing the use of the black and white
illustrations taken from Harrods catalogues.

Library of Congress Cataloging-in-Publication Data

Richardson, Rosamond.
    Harrods book of jams, jellies, and chutneys.

    1. Jam.   2. Jelly.   3. Chutney.   4. Harrods Ltd.
I. Harrods Ltd.   II. Title.
TX612.J3R53   1986   641.8′52   86-8019
ISBN 0-87795-838-6

Contents

Introduction

THERE is nothing quite like the personal satisfaction which comes from producing a wide range of home-made preserves – not only the making of them, but also the glorious sight of a pantry full of jams, jellies and chutneys. The satisfaction comes partly from mastering a craft, partly from knowing that you are utilizing a harvest to its full and partly from the joy of putting good food by for future use when the ingredients are no longer in season. Sometimes there is the added satisfaction of bringing the countryside into the kitchen, particularly during the late summer and early autumn when the hedgerows and fields bear their annual harvest of berries, nuts and mushrooms. These foods, all free for the picking, introduce new and interesting tastes to the palate, and open up an exciting range of original combinations to experiment with. The principal delight of this is that the activity involved – a pleasant country ramble rather than an expedition to the supermarket – is pleasurable and relaxing. By hoarding the fruits of the countryside, it gives us a chance to enjoy the misty, slightly chill days of early autumn as the sun sinks lower in the sky and winter draws on.

Your range of preserves can be as simple or as exotic as you choose: there is as much virtue in the simplest strawberry jam as in a mixed preserve using rare tropical fruits, or an unusual and delicately spiced chutney. For the adventurous cook who likes to experiment, however, the increasing availability of unusual fruits and vegetables makes for an exciting and creative challenge. Multicolored fruit and vegetables flown in fresh from all over the country are stacked high in gleaming piles, making our markets and supermarkets more exciting places than they have ever been before.

So here is a new range of unusual as well as simple recipes, ranging through jams both ordinary and extraordinary, and classic as well as unconventional marmalades. There are unusual jellies to go with both hot and cold meals, delicate fruit curds and cheeses, oriental chutneys and relishes, and crisp, tangy pickles, both sweet and sour, as well as some luxurious specialty conserves. The recipes utilize traditional ingredients as well as unusual combinations of exotic produce, fruit that can be gathered from the wild, and fruit and vegetables that you can grow yourself. With the loving care and artistry that goes into the skill of successful preserving, a new look at experimenting with novel combinations of fruits and vegetables, herbs and spices, flowers and leaves, will develop an intuition about mingling flavors and textures, as well as delighting the most demanding of palates.

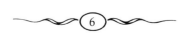

Jams

MAKING JAM is almost synonymous, for some people, with hominess, and indeed there is something about the seasonal smells as it is cooking and about the neat rows of glistening jars on the pantry shelf, that is both comforting and satisfying. Above all, though, the taste of home-made jam is quite incomparable with even the best brand names, and there are so many fruits to choose from nowadays that you can try out exciting new combinations that manufacturers have not yet thought of. Once the simple elements of jam-making have been mastered, it becomes a part of home-making which gives family and friends alike nostalgic memories through the years.

ESSENTIAL INGREDIENTS FOR JAM-MAKING

Fruit
The fruit should be firm and ripe, or just under-ripe, and always fresh and of good quality. Never use over-ripe fruit because, since the pectin in it is changing to pectin acid, the jam will not set. In a wet season, fruit has a lower sugar content than normal so there is an increased tendency to mildew and therefore less chance of long-term sound keeping. Always wash or rinse fruit before use to remove any traces of dust or dirt, and to clean off any chemicals with which it may have been treated. Remember that the grocer is not your only source of fruit – fruits from the garden and fruits from the countryside enhance the sense of satisfaction that is such an integral part of jam-making.

Sugar

Use refined, granulated cane or beet sugar unless a recipe specifies brown sugar or a syrup such as corn syrup, maple syrup or honey. Avoid the very dark sugars since they change the color of the fruit and tend to spoil its flavor. Sugar is a vital factor in the setting process, and the necessary level is between 55% and 70%, although a high acid content in the fruit makes the exact sugar balance less critical. If you warm the sugar slightly before stirring into the fruit, it will dissolve more quickly.

If your jam should crystallize during storage, this is due to either too much sugar, or to over-boiling; it also results if the storage place is too dry. You can employ a short-term remedy by turning the contents of the jar into a saucepan and heating gently to near-boiling point. Re-pot in a warm, clean jar. The jam will be satisfactory for immediate use; however, it will go sugary again sooner or later.

Pectin

Pectin is a natural, gum-like substance found in varying amounts in different fruits, usually in their cores, seeds or pits and skins. Its presence is essential to a good set in jams and jellies. Pectin content is particularly high in the seeds and white pith of citrus fruits, and in tart apples. There are some fruits which do not contain enough pectin and acid to provide a good set, so the answer is either to mix low pectin fruits with high pectin ones, or to add commercial pectin which can be bought in liquid or powder form. It substantially reduces the cooking time so is a labor-saving device if not an entirely economical one.

GUIDE TO THE PECTIN CONTENT OF FRUITS

HIGH	MEDIUM	LOW
tart cooking apples	fresh apricots	cherries
black currants	early blackberries	elderberries
cranberries	greengage plums	figs
damsons	loganberries	medlars
gooseberries	peaches	mulberries
lemons	plums	pears
grapefruit	raspberries	rhubarb
tart plums	sweet apples	strawberries
quinces		late blackberries
red currants		squash
loganberries		guavas
grapes		

ACID

Tartaric Acid
Tartaric acid is an organic acid common in plants, and found in especially high quantities in tart fruits. It is marketed in powdered form, and can be used to assist the setting of jams – to every 2 lb fruit used, dissolve 1 teaspoon tartaric acid in a little water and add to the pan at the end of the cooking process.

Citric Acid
Citric acid is a fairly weak organic acid found in the juice of lemons and other citrus fruits. It is a souring agent and preservative, and is available commercially in crystalline form. Pure lemon juice is also a good setting agent – use 2 tablespoons to every 2 lb fruit.

EQUIPMENT FOR JAM MAKING

Preserving Kettle

Choose a pan which will be large enough: it should not be more than half-full when the fruit and sugar are added, because they need to be able to boil rapidly without boiling over. Choose a heavy-bottomed aluminum or stainless steel pan for best results – never use iron or zinc pans because the acid in the fruit will attack the metal and the color and flavor of the jam will be destroyed. Enamel pans do not conduct heat fast enough for satisfactory jam-making and tend to burn easily; tin may melt! You can use a copper pan if you like, but be sure to remove all traces of polish before cooking the fruit, and be aware that much of the vitamin C content will be destroyed by its reaction with the metal. You'll also need a boiling water bath container for processing.

── ◆ OTHER EQUIPMENT ◆ ──

wooden spoons – long-handled for preference to ensure that they do not disappear beneath the simmering preserve. Metal spoons conduct heat too fast for comfortable handling and may be discolored by the acid.

large or nylon sieve or strainer – a metal sieve will impair the flavor of the preserve and can also be discolored by the acid in the fruit.

slotted spoon
sharp stainless steel knives for chopping and slicing the fruit
serrated knife
chopping board
juice squeezer
food mill or grinder with both fine and coarse blades AND/OR a
food processor
pitter for pitting fruit
wide-lipped jug for pouring
funnel
jelly thermometer
measuring cups and spoons, and ideally, household scales
double boiler for some curds etc.
plastic screw–top jars
jars with lids in prime condition
labels

BEST STRAWBERRY JAM (page 15)

BASIC METHOD

A jam is a preserve of fruit boiled with sugar and water, whereas a jelly is the fruit juice only boiled with sugar, and a marmalade is a kind of jam made with citrus fruits. Jams must have sufficient sugar for sound storage – organisms cannot grow when the sugar content is over 50%. Hence the addition of lemon juice in many recipes – its twofold purpose being to relieve the sweetness and to help with the set. Jams are usually cooked to 221°.

Remember that it is the fruit rather than the sugar that needs cooking, so jams and jellies boiled for too long with the sugar tend to lose color and flavor. Certainly soft fruits can be ruined by long boiling – they need just a short cooking time before the sugar is added.

To start with, smear a pat of butter over the bottom and sides of a preserving kettle before putting the fruit in – this will help prevent burning during the cooking process. An old country custom is to put a marble into the bottom of the pan for the same purpose (removing it before potting) – and it works!

Put the fruit into the pan, with or without water added as instructed in the recipe, and cook gently until the juices begin to run before bringing to boiling point. Simmer until the fruit is tender, then add the sugar – warmed for preference as it will dissolve more quickly. Stir over a gentle heat until the sugar has completely dissolved. Bring to a boil again and boil rapidly to setting point.

TESTING FOR DONENESS

Sheet Test

When the jam begins to thicken, dip in a wooden spoon and hold it over the pan. If, as the jam drops off the spoon, it forms a sheet and drops off as cleanly as a flake, then the jam will set when cold. If by any chance the jam fails to set, add 2 tablespoons lemon juice per 4 lb fruit and try again – or add commercial pectin in the quantity suggested on the label.

Refrigerator Test

When the jam starts to thicken, put a teaspoonful onto a cold saucer and put it in the refrigerator. Remove the pan of jam from the heat. Wait for 5 minutes, then tilt the saucer. If the jam wrinkles a little and does not run, it is ready for packing.

If it is still liquid and runs over the saucer, return the jam to the heat and continue boiling until the test is successful. Generally speaking, the stage of boiling the sugar to setting point takes about 10 minutes.

Thermometer

You will need a good cook's thermometer which goes up to and includes 220°. Always put a thermometer into hot water before use to prevent it cracking. To test for set, stir the jam so that the temperature is even throughout, and when the thermometer reads 220° a good set should be obtained – although in some cases 221–222° will be better. (Barometric pressure and altitude affect boiling point, so adjustments must be made for the weather and if over 1,000 feet above sea level.)

THE FINAL TOUCH

A pat of butter added just before the end of the cooking gives the jam a shine, and also makes scum easier to remove since it collects the scum in one place. Lift the scum off with a metal spoon and discard. If there are any more traces of scum, these are easily removed by dipping paper towels onto them and lifting off. A good jam will be stiff without being solid, clear and not cloudy, and have a good flavor. Preserves such as jams are best processed in a short boiling water bath (212°) before storage. Pack into jars, allowing ½ inch headroom, and complete seals after processing.

PACKING AND PROCESSING

Choose suitably sized canning jars – ½ and 1 pint jars are most convenient. Wash and rinse them thoroughly in scalding water. Keep the jars covered or filled with boiling water until ready for use. Pour or ladle the jam into the hot clean jar, leaving ½ inch headroom. Wipe carefully with a clean cloth wrung out in boiling water, then adjust the lids and process in a boiling water bath (212°) for 10 minutes. Complete the seals if necessary and let cool. Wipe the jars clean with a damp cloth and leave to dry. Label clearly, with the date as well as the contents, and store.

STORAGE

Choose a cool, dark, dry place: heat will shrink the contents of the jar, light will fade the color of the jam, and damp will encourage mold.

Raspberry and Rhubarb Jam

This delicious, summery jam is an unusual combination of two fruits which are often abundant at the same time. It is freshly sharp, a gorgeous pink color and a superb jam on freshly baked scones.

2 lb rhubarb   MAKES 5 lb
1 lb (3 cups) raspberries
⅔ cup water
3 lb (8 cups) sugar

Wash and cut the rhubarb into 1 inch lengths. Hull and rinse the raspberries.

Put the rhubarb into a preserving kettle with the water. Cover and simmer for about 10 minutes until tender. Remove the lid and boil fast to reduce to a thick pulp.

Add the raspberries to the pan with the sugar. Stir over a low heat until the sugar has dissolved. Bring to a boil and boil rapidly for about 10 minutes, stirring occasionally, or until setting point is reached.

Skim the jam, pack into hot, clean jars and cover. Process, complete seals and cool.

Gooseberry, Strawberry and Elderflower Jam

The exceptional and pungent flavor of elderflowers gives an exquisite taste to this mixture of two superb summer fruits. Together they combine to make an extraordinarily tasty and fragrant jam.

1½ lb (4 cups)   ⅔ cup water
  gooseberries   3 lb (8 cups) sugar
1½ lb (4⅔ cups)
  strawberries   MAKES 5 lb
6 large elderflower heads

Top, tail and wash the gooseberries. Hull and rinse the strawberries. Tie the elderflower heads in a cheesecloth bag.

Put the gooseberries in a preserving kettle with the water and bag of elderflowers. Simmer for about 15 minutes until the gooseberries are tender.

Add the strawberries to the pan and simmer for a further 3–4 minutes. Remove the bag of flowers and add the sugar. Stir over a low heat until the sugar has dissolved. Bring to a boil and boil rapidly for about 10 minutes, stirring occasionally, or until setting point is reached.

Skim the jam, pack into hot clean jars and cover. Process, complete seals and cool.

Summer Harvest Jam

This elegant jam is a celebration of the soft fruits of high summer. No matter which combination of berries you choose to use, the jam will be a lovely reminder of those sunny days.

4 lb (10–14 cups) mixed soft fruits, eg strawberries, raspberries, loganberries, red currants, black currants, gooseberries, etc.	5 lb (13 cups) sugar MAKES 8 lb

Hull and rinse the strawberries, raspberries and loganberries. Top, tail and wash the currants and gooseberries. Prepare any other fruits you may be using.

Put the fruit into a preserving kettle with a little water – the amount will depend on the ripeness of the fruit – and simmer for 5 minutes.

Add the sugar and stir over a low heat until dissolved. Bring to a boil and boil rapidly for about 10 minutes, stirring occasionally, or until setting point is reached.

Pack the jam into hot clean jars and cover. Process, complete seals and cool.

Best Strawberry Jam

Like most people, I like to make the most of the strawberry season while it is at its height. This jam, concocted under pressure of time one year, has become my family favorite and it honestly makes the best strawberry jam I have ever tasted. As with many of the low-pectin fruits, however, strawberry jam has a relatively short shelf-life, but that has never been a problem in my house – it vanishes all too quickly!

3 lb (9⅔ cups) strawberries 2 lb (5⅓ cups) sugar ⅔ cup water thick slice of lemon	MAKES 3–4 lb

Hull and rinse the strawberries. Put into a preserving kettle with the sugar, water and lemon slice. Simmer gently over a moderate heat until the sugar has dissolved. Bring to boil and boil rapidly for about 10 minutes, stirring occasionally, or until setting point is reached.

Skim the jam, pack into hot clean jars and cover. Process, complete seals and cool.

Black Currant and Cherry Jam

This dark, rich, mouthwatering combination of fruits fully lives up to its description. It is inspired by an idea from the original edition of Mrs. Beeton, who describes this jam as "very delicious."

2 lb (8 cups) black currants	2½ cups water
2 lb (4 cups) black cherries	3 lb (8 cups) sugar
	MAKES 5 lb

Wash the black currants. Wash and pit the cherries, removing the stalks.

Put the black currants into a preserving kettle with the water. Simmer very gently for 20–30 minutes. Strain through a jelly bag for 2–3 hours.

Put the cherries into the pan and cover with the black currant juice. Simmer for 10 minutes.

Add the sugar and stir over a moderate heat until dissolved. Bring to a boil and boil rapidly for about 10 minutes, stirring occasionally, or until setting point is reached.

Pack the jam into hot clean jars and cover. Process, complete seals and cool.

Fresh Peach Jam

This jam is as lovely as it sounds – delicate, with the soft texture of peach flesh and slightly sharp with the lemon juice. You could also infuse a rose geranium leaf in it during the cooking to give a special fragrance. Try this jam as a layer-cake filling – served with whipped cream, it makes a perfect dessert.

2 lb ripe peaches	MAKES 5 lb
⅔ cup water	
6 tablespoons lemon juice	
3 lb (8 cups) sugar	
1 cup liquid pectin	

Skin, pit and slice the peaches. Put into a preserving kettle with the water and lemon juice. Simmer gently for 10–15 minutes until tender.

Add the sugar and stir over a moderate heat until dissolved. Bring to a boil and boil rapidly for 10 minutes, stirring occasionally.

Remove from the heat, stir in the pectin and then bring back to a steady boil for a further 5 minutes.

Allow to cool for a few minutes. Pack the jam into hot clean jars and cover. Process, complete seals and cool.

Hedgerow Jam

Berrying and nutting in the late days of summer, as warm days give way to autumnal mists, have provided me with many contented moments. This jam, which is a rich combination of wild fruits and nuts, all harvested for free along a country walk, makes a delightful addition to the pantry shelf.

1 lb (2 cups) elderberries	¾ cups shelled walnuts
1 lb crab apples	7½ cups water
1 lb (1 cup) blackberries	5 lb (13 cups) sugar
1 lb wild plums (such as damsons)	
2 cups shelled hazelnuts	MAKES 8 lb

Strip the elderberries off their stalks and rinse. Wash, core and chop the crab apples. Hull and rinse the blackberries. Wash, pit and chop the wild plums. Coarsely chop the nuts.

Put the fruit into a preserving kettle with the water. Simmer for 15 minutes.

Add the sugar and stir over a moderate heat until dissolved. Bring to a boil and boil rapidly. After 5 minutes, add the nuts and continue boiling for about 10 minutes, stirring occasionally, or until setting point is reached.

Skim if necessary, pack into hot clean jars and cover. Process, complete seals and cool.

Jam of Green Figs

Fresh figs always strike me as being the most luscious of fruits – warm with sunshine, dripping with juice and soft in texture. Their delicate and quite distinctive taste makes a marvelous, thick jam, as good on breads and scones as in desserts and tarts.

1½ lb ripe green figs	rind and juice of
2 lb rhubarb	2 lemons
3 lb (8 cups) sugar	
	MAKES 6 lb

Wipe the figs and remove the stems, then roughly chop. Rinse and cut the rhubarb into 1-inch lengths.

Put the figs and rhubarb in a double boiler and cover with the sugar. Put on the lid and cook over boiling water for about 30–40 minutes until the sugar has dissolved in the juices and the fruit is quite soft.

Transfer the mixture to a preserving kettle with the lemon rind and juice, stirring well. Bring to a boil and boil rapidly for about 10 minutes, stirring occasionally, or until setting point is reached.

Pack the jam into hot clean jars and cover. Process, complete seals and cool.

Cherry and Apricot Jam

If you can lay your hands on a little gadget that pits cherries and other small fruits, it will take much of the drudgery out of making this jam and will encourage you to take full advantage of the cherry crop while it is in full season. I love apricots in jam, and this delightful combination of fruit is superlative.

1 lb (2 cups) cherries	3 lb (8 cups) sugar
2 lb apricots	juice of 2 lemons
⅔ cup water	
	MAKES 5 lb

Wash and pit the cherries, removing the stalks. Wash, pit and slice the apricots.

Put the cherries and apricots into a preserving kettle with the water and simmer for about 10–12 minutes until the fruit is tender.

Add the sugar and lemon juice and stir over a gentle heat until the sugar has dissolved. Bring to a boil and boil rapidly for about 10 minutes, stirring occasionally, or until setting point is reached.

Pack the jam into hot clean jars and cover. Process, complete seals and cool.

DRIED APRICOT AND ALMOND JAM (page 20)

Dried Apricot and Almond Jam

A great favorite with family and friends alike, this is a jam of great sophistication and yet so simple to make. The flavor of the almonds comes through in a subtle yet amazing way and, of course, their crunch is in delectable contrast to the soft, sweet apricots. It also has a translucent quality which makes it even more appetizing.

1½ lb (4½ cups) dried
  apricot halves
5 pints water
¾ cup blanched almonds

juice of 2 lemons
2 lb (5⅓ cups) sugar

MAKES 5 lb

Rinse the apricots and soak overnight in the water. Drain the apricots, reserving the soaking water, and roughly chop. Roughly chop the almonds.

Lightly butter a preserving kettle, then add the apricots, soaking water and lemon juice. Simmer for 20 minutes, stirring frequently.

Add the sugar and stir over a medium heat until dissolved. Stir in the almonds, bring to a boil and boil rapidly for about 10 minutes, stirring occasionally, or until setting point is reached.

Pack into hot clean jars and cover. Process, complete seals and cool.

Pear and Ginger Jam

This is a jam of finesse, unbeatable on slices of freshly baked bread. The touch of hot spiciness in the ginger is in perfect balance with the delicacy of the pears, and makes a truly elegant and original jam. It has a thin, runny texture which is a part of its charm.

2 lb pears
4 oz (½ cup) preserved
  ginger
2 lb (5⅓ cups) sugar
1¼ cups water

1 oz (1-inch) fresh ginger
juice of 2 lemons

MAKES 2 lb

Peel, core and dice the pears. Cut the preserved ginger into small chunks.

Put all the ingredients into a preserving kettle and stir over a gentle heat until the sugar has dissolved. Bring to a boil and boil rapidly for about 10 minutes, stirring occasionally, or until setting point is reached.

Remove the piece of fresh ginger, lift out the fruit with a slotted spoon and place in hot clean jars. Rapidly boil the syrup to reduce for a few minutes, then pour over the fruit to cover. Cover and process, then complete seals and cool.

Carrot and Almond Jam

Most people are astonished at the idea of carrots in jam, but it was a common practice in the 19th century. Mrs Beeton used to make it as an imitation apricot jam. Its sweetness and bright coloring make a perfect jam, and the taste and texture of almonds give this recipe extra flavor and crunch. The jam will not keep without the addition of the brandy – which has the pleasing side effect of lifting the jam into the realms of the extra-special.

5 cups grated carrots	grated rind of 2 lemons
¾ cup blanched almonds	juice of 4 lemons
3 lb (8 cups) sugar	¼ cup brandy

MAKES 5 lb

Chop the almonds.

Put the carrots into a saucepan of boiling water and cook for 15–20 minutes.

Drain and blend to a purée with a little of the cooking water.

Put the carrot purée into a preserving kettle with the sugar, lemon rind and juice, stirring until the sugar has dissolved. Simmer gently for 5 minutes until the mixture begins to thicken. Stir in the almonds and brandy.

Pack into hot clean jars and cover. Process, complete seals and cool.

Scented Lychee Jam

Exotic tropical fruits are so easily available nowadays that it is rather fun to make preserves with them for a change. Lychees have a beautiful texture and color, and their delicacy of taste is highlighted here by the flavor of rose geranium leaves and a few almonds.

1½ lb fresh lychees	5 tablespoons water
3 rose geranium leaves	½ cup slivered almonds
2⅔ cups sugar	
juice of 1 lemon	MAKES 2 lb

Shell and seed the lychees. Tie the rose geranium leaves in a cheesecloth bag.

Put all the ingredients into a preserving kettle. Stir over a moderate heat until the sugar has dissolved. Bring to a boil and boil rapidly for about 10 minutes to a thick syrup, stirring frequently. Continue boiling for about 10 minutes, stirring occasionally, or until setting point is reached.

Pack into hot clean jars and cover. Process, complete seals and cool.

Raisin, Date and Banana Jam

This is a tour de force, a really gastronomic assembling of ingredients which combine to make a fantastic jam. It is wonderful with breakfast toast, lovely in almond pastry slices and delicious spread on crêpes. A must for the pantry.

½ lb (1½ cups) dried apricots	3 cups sliced bananas
1 lb (2⅔ cups) raisins	4 lb (10⅔ cups) sugar
1 lb dates	MAKES 5 lb

Rinse the apricots. Cover the raisins and apricots with water and soak overnight. Pit and chop the dates.

Put all the fruit into a preserving kettle, with the soaking water. Simmer for 15 minutes.

Add the sugar and stir over a moderate heat until dissolved. Bring to a boil and boil rapidly for about 10 minutes, stirring occasionally, or until setting point is reached.

Pack the jam into hot clean jars and cover. Process, complete seals and cool.

MELON AND PINEAPPLE JAM (page 24)

Melon and Pineapple Jam

Two tropical fruits, with the addition of lemon juice to provide extra flavor, make this translucent and succulent jam. Pale golden and gleaming, it is a beautiful sight among a range of preserves in the pantry. I use this jam a great deal in desserts of all kinds.

3 lb honeydew melon	juice of 3 lemons
1½ lb fresh pineapple	3 lb (8 cups) sugar

MAKES 5 lb

Cut the melon in half, scoop out the seeds and cut the flesh into small cubes, yielding about 2 lb (6 cups). Remove the skin from the pineapple and cut out the central core, then cut the flesh into small chunks.

Put the melon and pineapple into a preserving kettle with the lemon juice. Simmer gently for 10–15 minutes until tender.

Add the sugar and stir over a moderate heat until dissolved. Bring to a boil and boil rapidly for about 10 minutes, stirring occasionally, or until setting point is reached.

Pack the jam into hot clean jars and cover. Process, complete seals and cool.

Apricot, Walnut and Pineapple Jam

I love nuts in jam. It is not just their contrasting texture, but also the fact that the cooking at high temperature brings out the finest in their taste. Pineapple makes a marvelous jam – silky and transparent and, in combination with apricots, makes a jam to remember.

1 lb ripe apricots	1 cup walnut pieces
1 lb (2⅔ cups) sugar	
8 oz can pineapple	MAKES 2–3 lb
chunks, in natural juice	

Rinse, halve and pit the apricots. Place in a bowl and cover them with the sugar. Leave to stand for 2 hours.

Meanwhile, crack the pits and remove the kernels. Drain the pineapple chunks and reserve the juice. Chop the walnuts.

Put the apricots, sugar and pineapple juice into a preserving kettle and gradually bring to a boil, stirring constantly and skimming as necessary.

Add the pineapple chunks, kernels and walnuts. Simmer very gently for about 10 minutes, stirring occasionally, or until setting point is reached.

Pack into hot clean jars and cover. Process, complete seals and cool.

Banana and Dried Fig Jam

I was fascinated to try this unusual mixture of fresh and dried fruit. My experiment was richly rewarded by an exotic, thickly textured jam which turned out to be utterly scrumptious – quite irresistible on the tea-table, and now a regular feature in my pantry.

4 lemons	⅔ cups water
3½ lb bananas	3 lb (8 cups) sugar
½ lb (1½ cups) dried figs	
	MAKES 5 lb

Peel the rind and pith from the lemons. Remove the seeds and put the seeds and pith in a cheesecloth bag. Peel and cut the bananas into ¼-inch slices. Chop the figs.

Put the banana slices into a bowl with the water and the juice of two of the lemons. Add the bag of seeds and the figs. Cover with the sugar and leave to stand for 24 hours.

Transfer the banana mixture to a preserving kettle and heat gently until the sugar has dissolved. Bring to a boil and boil rapidly for about 10 minutes, stirring occasionally, or until setting point is reached. Remove the cheesecloth bag.

Pack the jam into hot clean jars and cover. Process, complete seals and cool.

Squash, Pineapple and Ginger Jam

This golden jam, which gleams as the light shines through it, has been a family favorite for years. It is wonderfully, even unashamedly, sweet, yet the ginger counteracts this with its characteristic bite. This is a marvelous filling for cakes and crêpes as well as being the devil's own temptation on fresh bread.

6 lb peeled and seeded zucchini or chayote cut into small cubes (about 18 cups)	1 cup sliced preserved ginger
	6 lb (16 cups) sugar
1 lb peeled and cored pineapple, cut into little chunks (2 cups)	MAKES 10 lb

Mix the squash and pineapple together and make alternating layers of fruit and sugar in a preserving kettle. Leave overnight to extract the juice.

Bring to a boil and boil rapidly for 15–20 minutes to reduce the liquid. Add the ginger and boil rapidly for about 10 minutes, stirring occasionally, or until setting point is reached.

Pack into hot clean jars and cover. Process, complete seals and cool.

Rosy Tomato Jam

The unusual combination of tomatoes and lemons makes a jam with a quite distinctive character – although it's not really a jam at all, more like a relish. I like to use it in toasted cheese sandwiches – it transforms them!

5 lemons, washed	pat of butter
¼ pint water	
2 lb ripe tomatoes	MAKES 3 lb
2 lb (5⅓ cups) sugar	

Cut the lemons in half and squeeze the juice, reserving the pits. Remove the remaining flesh from the lemon halves and reserve. Cut the excess pith away from the lemon rind and cut the zest into thin strips. Place in a saucepan, add the water and simmer, covered, for 20 minutes.

Skin and quarter the tomatoes then remove the cores and seeds and tie in a piece of cheesecloth with the lemon pits and flesh. Measure the lemon juice, adding enough water to yield 3 pints. Pour into a preserving pan. Coarsely chop the tomato flesh and add to the pan with the softened lemon shreds, liquid and cheesecloth bag. Simmer gently for about 40 minutes until tender. Remove the cheesecloth bag and squeeze it well, allowing the juice to run back into the pan. Remove the pan from the heat, add the sugar, stirring until dissolved then add a pat of butter and boil rapidly for 20 minutes or until setting point is reached. Take the pan off the heat and remove any scum with a slotted spoon. Pot the jam in warm, clean jars and cover. Seal immediately.

Blueberry Jam

The prettiness of this jam is immensely appealing – the berries just manage to hold their shape and not become too pulpy, and the jam is scrumptious with freshly baked bread at tea time. So when the blueberry is available, make the most of it and enjoy this jam!

2½ lb blueberries	pat of butter
¼ pint water	225 ml (8 fl oz) pectin
45 ml (3 tbsp) lemon juice	
3 lb sugar	MAKES ABOUT 5½ lb

Wash the blueberries then put them into a preserving pan with the water and lemon juice. Simmer gently for 10–15 minutes until the fruit is soft and just beginning to pulp. Remove the pan from the heat, add the sugar, stir until dissolved, then add a pat of butter. Bring to the boil and boil rapidly for 3 minutes. Remove the pan from the heat, add the pectin, return to the heat and boil for a further minute. Allow to cool slightly before potting the jam in warm, clean jars. Cover and seal while still hot.

Jellies

ALWAYS think that making jellies is simpler than any other preserve-making, so long as you have a jelly-bag and a thermometer! You don't have to skin or core or top and tail the fruits, and the basic rules about the ratio of juice to sugar remain constant, so after a while you can do it almost automatically. Jellies look so beautiful in the jars, too, translucent and shining, all with delicate colors, whether pale or dark. Jellies can be used to go with both savory and sweet recipes, and are perennially useful and popular with young and old alike. And you can make a jelly from almost anything – from tomatoes to rose-hips, green peppers to blackberries, and all are delicious.

◆ SPECIAL EQUIPMENT ◆

In addition to the basic equipment needed for jam-making, (see page 10), you will need a jelly bag or a linen cloth for straining the juice from the cooked fruit. Cleanliness is paramount at this stage: always scald the cloth or the jelly bag in boiling water before use, then wring it dry. The traditional way to suspend a cloth or jelly bag is to use an upturned kitchen stool. To do this, tie the four corners of the linen cloth very securely (because of the weight of the fruit and water) to the four legs. Place a bowl underneath and allow the juice to drip through, undisturbed, for 12 hours. With a jelly bag, tie the suspending tapes to the bars of the stool. Do not be tempted to squeeze the bag in order to extract the maximum juice – this will turn the jelly cloudy.

◆ BASIC METHOD ◆

Make sure that the fruit you are using is clean, and not over-ripe. Remove any stalks but it is not necessary to top and tail berries such as gooseberries and currants. Pick the fruit over and discard any moldy or over-ripe ones. It is best to pick the fruit on a dry day, because fruit sodden with rain will attract mildew. Rinse the fruit to remove any dirt or grit; the fruit is then ready to cook as instructed in the recipe.

The juice is then strained through the scalded jelly bag or linen cloth (see above), and measured. The general rule for jellies is to add 1 lb (2⅔ cups) sugar to every 2½ cups juice. This gives a jelly which will both set and keep, although this ratio varies slightly in recipes for different fruits. Stir over a medium heat until dissolved, then bring to a boil and boil fast to setting point. This will take about 10 minutes, longer if the fruit has a high water content. As a guide, about 10 lb jelly will result from every 6 lb (16 cups) sugar used.

Skim the jelly with a metal spoon and remove the last traces of scum with a piece of paper towel. A thick, fairly sticky juice is sure to contain plenty of pectin, but the testing for doneness is the same as that for jam (see page 12). Pour immediately into hot sterile jars, before it has a chance to set in the pan. Cover at once with melted paraffin wax, or with 2-piece screwband lids if using modern jelly jars. Store in a cool, dry, dark place.

Suitable Fruits for Jelly-Making

Apples, barberries, blackberries – both red and ripe, black currants, boysenberries, cherries, cranberries, gooseberries, raspberries, strawberries, crab apples, elderberries, loganberries, mulberries, plums, pears, quinces, red and white currants, sloes, rose-hips, oranges.

Flavorings for Jellies

Aromatic leaves and petals give a delicate and unusual flavor to jellies – for example a scented geranium leaf gives apple jelly a beautiful taste and aroma. You can use peach leaves for their almondy flavor, lemon verbena for its lemony perfume, red scented rose petals, mint leaves, angelica leaves or stem – all add their distinctive and characteristic flavors to make a jelly with a difference. As a general rule, use one highly scented leaf or a small handful of petals to each 2½ cups juice – in both cases tied in a cheesecloth bag and suspended from the pan handle while the jelly is boiling to setting point.

Making Jelly in a Pressure Cooker

To save time, you can cook the fruit for making jellies in a pressure cooker, as indeed you can with jams. First wash the fruit, then put it into the pan, making sure that it does not fill up to more than halfway. As a general rule, pressure cook berries at 10 lb pressure for 5 minutes. Fruits such as rose hips will need 30 minutes, whereas apples will take only 8 minutes. Follow your manufacturers' instructions.

Mash the fruit, then strain through a jelly bag in the normal way. Continue the cooking process as for the preserving kettle technique on page 12.

Serving Ideas

Jellies make a tasty accompaniment to roast meats both hot and cold, and certain ones are delicious with cheeses. A lunch of bread and cheese is enhanced by a selection of sweet and sharp jellies, and they go beautifully with cream cheese, too. Fold a scented jelly into yogurt to sweeten and flavor.

Quantities

Exact quantities of jelly vary with the water content of the fruit and the length of time needed to cook them. As a general rule, 10 lb jelly is made from each 6 lb (16 cups) sugar used.

Black Currant Jelly

The strong, rich taste of black currants makes, to my mind, the king of jellies. A beautiful dark red, almost black, in color, it is so versatile too – you can use black currant jelly in desserts and pies, as a spread, or with cold cuts. An essential standby for a well-stocked pantry.

4 lb (16 cups) ripe black currants	2½ cups water sugar

Wash and strip the black currants off their stalks but do not top and tail them.

Put the black currants into a preserving kettle with the water. Cover and simmer for 30 minutes, crushing the fruit from time to time with the back of a wooden spoon. Allow to cool a little in the pan, then strain through a jelly bag overnight.

Measure the juice into the cleaned preserving kettle. To every 2½ cups juice, add 2⅔ cups sugar. Stir over a gentle heat until the sugar has dissolved. Bring to a boil and boil rapidly for about 10 minutes, stirring occasionally, or until setting point is reached, removing the scum as it forms on the surface.

Pour the jelly into hot sterile jars and seal immediately.

Apricot Muscatel Jelly

The unusual idea of including muscat raisins in jelly-making works very well. They add their distinctive taste to that of the apricots, making a jelly that is as delicious in savory as in sweet dishes.

1 lb (3 cups) dried apricots	⅔ cup muscatel wine sugar
4 oz (1 cup) muscat raisins	¾ cup liquid pectin
7½ cups water	
juice of 2 lemons	

Rinse the apricots and raisins. Cover them with the water and leave to soak for 48 hours.

Put the apricots and raisins into a preserving kettle with the soaking water and lemon juice. Simmer for about 25 minutes until the fruit is very soft. Strain through a jelly bag overnight.

Add the wine to the juice and measure into the cleaned preserving kettle. To every 2½ cups juice, add 2⅔ cups sugar. Stir over a gentle heat until the sugar has dissolved. Bring to a boil and boil rapidly for 10 minutes. Add the pectin and stir in thoroughly.

Skim if necessary, pour the jelly into hot sterile jars and seal immediately.

Cranberry Wine Jelly

This is a bright red jelly in the classical style, beautifully sharp and an excellent foil for rich meats such as lamb or game birds.

2 lb (6 cups) cranberries	sugar
1¼ cups water	1¼ cups dry red wine

Wash the cranberries. Put into a preserving kettle with the water. Cover and simmer gently for about 25 minutes, until tender. Strain through a jelly bag overnight.

Measure the juice into the cleaned preserving kettle. To every 2½ cups juice, add 2 cups sugar. Stir over a gentle heat until the sugar has dissolved. Add the wine. Bring to a boil and boil rapidly for about 10 minutes, stirring occasionally, or until setting point is reached.

Skim, pour the jelly into hot sterile jars and seal immediately.

Grape Burgundy Jelly

The delicate flavor of grapes makes a lovely jelly, and the touch of red wine gives this luxury recipe a certain quality, as well as a beautiful magenta color. It is delicious on fresh bread or toast, and is also an interesting accompaniment to hot roast meats.

1½ lb ripe purple grapes	⅔ cup dry red wine
1¼ cups water	1 cup liquid pectin
sugar	
2 tablespoons lemon juice	

Wash, seed and crush the grapes, about one-third at a time, in a food processor for a few seconds.

Put the grapes into a preserving kettle with the water. Cover and simmer for 20 minutes. Strain through a jelly bag overnight.

Measure the juice into the cleaned preserving kettle. To every 2½ cups juice, add 2 cups sugar. Stir in the lemon juice and wine. Stir over a gentle heat until the sugar has dissolved. Bring to a boil and simmer for 15 minutes. Remove from the heat and stir in the pectin. Skim if necessary, pour the jelly into hot sterile jars and seal.

MANY BERRY JELLY (page 36)

Blackberry and Gooseberry Jelly

This unusual mixture of late summer fruits makes a really wonderful dark red jelly. Delicious at breakfast time, it gets the day off to a flying start!

2 lb (8 cups) blackberries	2 cups water
1 lb (2⅔ cups) gooseberries	sugar

Rinse the blackberries and gooseberries. Put the fruit into a preserving kettle with the water. Cover and simmer for 30–40 minutes until completely soft. Strain through a jelly bag overnight.

Measure the juice into the cleaned preserving kettle. To every 2½ cups juice, add 2⅔ cups sugar. Stir over a gentle heat until the sugar has dissolved. Bring to a boil and boil rapidly for about 10 minutes, stirring occasionally, or until setting point is reached.

Skim, pour the jelly into hot sterile jars and seal immediately.

Mulberry Jelly

The mulberry is an exquisite fruit, dripping with deep red juice which stains the fingers like ink. It is, however, full of pits so making a jelly is the obvious and best way to make the most of its unique flavor.

1 lb (3 cups) mulberries	⅔ cup water
1 large tart apple	sugar

Rinse the mulberries. Wash and chop the apple. Put the fruit into a preserving kettle with the water. Cover and simmer gently for 30 minutes until the fruit is very soft. Strain the fruit mixture through a jelly bag overnight.

Measure the juice into the cleaned preserving pan. To every 2½ cups juice, add 2⅔ cups sugar. Stir over a gentle heat until the sugar has dissolved. Bring to a boil and boil rapidly for about 10 minutes, stirring occasionally, or until setting point is reached.

Skim, pour the jelly into hot sterile jars and seal immediately.

Raspberry Jelly

Nothing can beat homemade raspberry jelly on a tea-table piled high with fresh scones and newly baked bread. So when raspberries reach their peak in the summer, this is one of the nicest ways to preserve them.

4 lb (13 cups) raspberries
2½ cups water
sugar

Hull and rinse the raspberries. Put into a preserving kettle with the water. Cover and simmer gently for 25 minutes. Allow to cool a little in the pan, then strain through a jelly bag overnight.

Measure the juice into the cleaned preserving kettle. To every 2½ cups juice, add 2⅔ cups sugar. Stir over a moderate heat until the sugar has dissolved. Bring to a boil and boil rapidly for about 10 minutes, stirring occasionally, or until setting point is reached.

Skim, pour the jelly into hot sterile jars and seal immediately.

Tangerine and Grapefruit Jelly

This wonderful citrus jelly is a clear, pale gold in color and has a sharp, clean taste which personally I love. For those who enjoy slightly bitter flavors, this is gorgeous on toast, and superlative with hot roast chicken or other poultry.

| 2 grapefruit | 1 lemon |
| 2 tangerines | sugar |

Wash and coarsely chop the fruit. Put into a preserving kettle with water to cover. Cover and simmer for 2 hours. Strain through a jelly bag overnight.

Measure the juice into the cleaned preserving kettle. To every 2½ cups juice, add 2⅔ cups sugar. Stir over a gentle heat until the sugar has dissolved. Bring to a boil and boil rapidly for about 10 minutes, stirring occasionally, or until setting point is reached.

Pour the jelly into hot sterile jars and seal immediately.

Tropical Fruit Jelly

When the markets are full of tropical fruits, it is fun to make up new combinations and branch out from traditional jelly-making. Selections from any of these succulent fruits will make a range of fragrant and interesting jellies. Use a selection of some of the following:

nectarines, mangoes, guavas, papayas, lychees, kiwi, persimmons, cantaloupe, pineapple	sugar lemon juice

Rinse and prepare all the fruit. For example, quarter the nectarines, mangoes, guavas and papayas (you can leave the seeds and pits in); peel the lychees and kiwifruit; chop the persimmons; scoop out the flesh from the melons and pineapple, then roughly chop.

Put the fruit into a preserving kettle with water to cover. Cover and simmer for 30 minutes. Strain through a jelly bag overnight.

Measure the juice into the cleaned preserving kettle. To every 2½ cups juice, add 2⅔ cups sugar and 1 tablespoon lemon juice. Stir over a gentle heat until the sugar has dissolved. Bring to a boil and boil rapidly for about 10 minutes, stirring occasionally, or until setting point is reached.

Pour the jelly into hot sterile jars and seal immediately.

Rose Petal Jelly

Scented rose petals give a fantastic flavor to a fruit jelly – it is a pity that we do not use them more than we do in cooking. They did in the old days and for good reason: they make something very special out of something very simple.

2 lb tart apples	2 oz (1–1½ cups) dark red
3 cups water	scented rose petals
juice of 1 lemon	sugar

Wash and roughly chop the apples. Put into a preserving kettle with 2½ cups of the water and the lemon juice. Cover and simmer gently for about 30 minutes until pulpy. Strain through a jelly bag overnight.

Meanwhile, cut the triangular white base from the rose petals and discard. Put the petals into the kettle with the remaining water. Cover and simmer for 15 minutes. Strain through a jelly bag separately, or use a piece of clean linen or cheesecloth.

Mix the two juices together and measure them into the cleaned preserving kettle. To every 2½ cups juice, add 2 cups sugar. Stir over a gentle heat until the sugar has dissolved. Bring to a boil and boil rapidly for about 10 minutes, stirring occasionally, or until setting point is reached.

Skim, pour the jelly into hot sterile jars and seal immediately.

ROSE PETAL JELLY (above)

Many Berry Jelly

When the soft fruit harvest is at its peak, this is a gorgeous way of combining them – their tastes mingle and yet are not lost. This is a jelly to remind you of long summer days later on in the year when these fruits are no longer around.

Equal quantities of
cherries
raspberries
strawberries
gooseberries
sugar

Wash and pit the cherries, removing the stems. Hull and rinse the raspberries and strawberries. Wash the gooseberries. Put the fruit into a large strong bowl. Cover with a plate and weigh it down with a heavy bowl or something similar to crush the fruit. Leave overnight.

Put the fruit into a preserving kettle with all the extracted juice and enough water to cover. Simmer for 10 minutes. Strain through a jelly bag overnight.

Measure the juice into the cleaned preserving kettle. To every 2½ cups juice, add 2 cups sugar. Stir over a gentle heat until the sugar has dissolved. Bring to a boil and boil rapidly for about 10 minutes, stirring occasionally, or until setting point is reached.

Skim, pour the jelly into hot sterile jars and seal immediately.

Guava Jelly

Tropical guavas make a beautiful soft pink jelly, which looks lovely among a range of multicolored jams and jellies on the pantry shelf.

guavas
sugar
lime juice

Wash and cut the guavas into quarters. Put into a preserving kettle with enough water just to cover. Cover and simmer for 30 minutes. Strain through a jelly bag overnight.

Measure the juice back into the cleaned preserving kettle. To every 2½ cups juice, add 2 cups sugar and 1 tablespoon lime juice. Stir over a medium heat until the sugar has dissolved. Bring to a boil and boil rapidly for about 10 minutes, stirring occasionally, or until setting point is reached.

Skim, pour the jelly into hot sterile jars and seal immediately.

Red and White Currant Jelly

This fine jelly has a delicate flavor and lovely deep pink color. It goes particularly well with game birds, its strength and sharpness providing the perfect balance to their richness.

3 lb (12 cups) white currants	1 quart water
3 lb (12 cups) red currants	sugar

Strip the currants from the stalks and place in a colander. Gently rinse under cold running water and shake thoroughly to drain.

Put the fruit into a preserving kettle with the water. Bring slowly to a boil, mashing the fruit occasionally with the back of a wooden spoon to break it up. Cover and simmer gently for 30 minutes. Strain through a jelly bag overnight.

Measure the juice into the cleaned preserving kettle. To every 2½ cups juice, add 2⅔ cups sugar. Stir over a gentle heat until the sugar has dissolved. Bring to a boil and boil rapidly for about 10 minutes, stirring occasionally, or until setting point is reached.

Skim, pour the jelly into hot sterile jars and seal immediately.

Medlar Jelly

The medlar is an Old World fruit, unpromising to look at – rather like a large, russet-colored rose hip with rough, leathery skin – but much used in the past by the country housewife as part of her wild harvest. Making jelly with these quince-like fruits is the best way of using them.

4 lb medlars	1 quart water
4 lemons	sugar

Wash and roughly chop the medlars. Peel the lemons and squeeze the juice. Put the lemon rinds into a preserving kettle with the medlars and water. Cover and simmer for 1 hour until the fruit is thoroughly softened. Strain through a jelly bag overnight.

Measure the juice into the cleaned preserving kettle. To every 2½ cups juice, add 2⅔ cups sugar. Add the lemon juice. Stir over a gentle heat until the sugar has dissolved. Bring to a boil and boil rapidly for about 10 minutes, stirring occasionally, or until setting point is reached.

Skim, pour the jelly into hot sterile jars and seal immediately.

Crab Apple and Thyme Jelly

A sharp, aromatic jelly in which the thyme gives its pungent flavor and aroma to a sharp, clear red jelly. It is delicious with the Thanksgiving turkey as a change from the traditional cranberry sauce or jelly.

3 lb crab apples
large bunch of thyme
sugar

Wash the crab apples. Put in a preserving kettle with water to cover and the thyme. Cover and simmer for 40 minutes. Strain through a jelly bag overnight.

Measure the juice into the cleaned preserving kettle. To every 2½ cups juice, add 2⅔ cups sugar. Stir over a gentle heat until the sugar has dissolved. Bring to a boil and boil rapidly for about 10 minutes, stirring occasionally, or until setting point is reached.

Skim, pour the jelly into hot sterile jars and seal immediately.

Rose Geranium and Orange Jelly

The simple device of adding a scented leaf to fruit while it is cooking gives an utterly distinctive flavor and aroma to jelly. Rose geranium with orange is one of the most exquisite of combinations.

2 lb oranges	sugar
1 quart water	1 cup liquid pectin
4–5 rose geranium leaves	

Wash and halve the oranges. Squeeze the juice, then roughly chop the fruit. Put into a preserving kettle with the water. Cover and simmer for 1½–2 hours until the rind is soft, adding the rose geranium leaves for the last 10 minutes of the cooking. Strain through the jelly bag overnight, leaving the leaves in the pulp.

Measure the juice into the cleaned preserving kettle. To every 2½ cups juice, add 2⅔ cups sugar. Stir over a gentle heat until the sugar has dissolved. Bring to a boil and boil rapidly for 15 minutes. Remove from the heat, add the pectin and stir well.

Skim if necessary, pour the jelly into hot sterile jars and seal immediately.

CRAB APPLE AND THYME JELLY (above left)

Sage and Apple Jelly

Herb jellies make marvelous companions to meat dishes, both hot and cold. This combination of sage and apple goes particularly well with pork.

2 lb tart apples	pared rind and juice of
large bunch of fresh sage	1 lemon
	sugar

Wash and roughly chop the apples. Put into a preserving kettle with water to cover, the bunch of sage, lemon rind and juice. Cover and simmer for about 30 minutes until the fruit is very soft. Strain the fruit mixture through a jelly bag overnight.

Measure the juice into the cleaned preserving kettle. To every 2½ cups juice, add 2⅔ cups sugar. Stir over a gentle heat until the sugar has dissolved. Bring to a boil and boil rapidly for about 10 minutes, stirring occasionally, or until setting point is reached.

Skim, pour the jelly into hot sterile jars and seal immediately.

Pear and Rosemary Jelly

This is a delicate and beautifully balanced jelly. They say that rosemary is for remembrance and this is definitely a taste to remember!

2 lb pears	sugar
pared rind and juice of	1 cup liquid pectin
2 lemons	
medium bunch of fresh	
rosemary	

Wash and remove the stalks from the pears and chop the fruit roughly. Put into a preserving kettle with the lemon rind and juice and bunch of rosemary. Add enough water just to cover the fruit. Cover and simmer for 25–30 minutes until the pears are very soft. Strain through a jelly bag overnight.

Measure the juice into the cleaned preserving kettle. To every 2½ cups juice, add 2⅔ cups sugar. Stir over a gentle heat until the sugar has dissolved. Bring to a boil and boil rapidly for 10 minutes. Remove from the heat and add the pectin, stirring in well.

Skim if necessary, pour the jelly into hot sterile jars and seal immediately.

Mint Jelly

This famous sauce was, so some say, invented by the Romans to go with roast lamb – both to counteract its richness and to complement its taste. Whoever's idea it was, it has lasted and become a classic of English cookery.

5 lb cooking apples	sugar
2 pints water	6–8 tbsp chopped fresh
few sprigs of fresh mint	mint
2 pints white vinegar	few drops of green food
	coloring (optional)

Wash the apples and remove any bruised or damaged portions. Roughly chop them into thick chunks without peeling or coring. Place them in a large saucepan with the water and mint sprigs. Bring to the boil, then simmer gently for about 45 minutes until soft and pulpy. Stir from time to time to prevent sticking. Add the vinegar and boil for a further 5 minutes.

Strain through a jelly bag overnight.

Measure the juice and put it in a preserving pan with 1 lb sugar for each 20 oz juice. Stir over a gentle heat until the sugar has dissolved, then boil rapidly for about 10 minutes until setting point is reached. Take the pan off the heat and remove any scum with a slotted spoon. Stir in the chopped mint and add a few drops of green food coloring, if liked. Allow to cool slightly, then stir well to distribute the mint. Pour the jelly into warm, clean jars and cover. Seal immediately.

Bitter Lime Jelly with Pernod

This sophisticated and elegant jelly never fails to win admiring comments. Served with charcuterie as an hors d'oeuvre, it makes an original and mouthwatering start to a meal, it is also excellent with roast game birds.

4 limes	sugar
6 pints water	1 tbsp Pernod

Wash the limes and roughly slice them. Put the limes in a preserving pan with the water and simmer gently for 1 hour until the fruit is soft. Strain overnight through a jelly bag into a large bowl.

Measure the extract and return it to the pan with 1 lb sugar for each 20 oz extract. Stir over a gentle heat until the sugar has dissolved. Bring to the boil and boil rapidly for 10–15 minutes or until setting point is reached. Take the pan off the heat and stir in the Pernod. Remove any scum from the surface with a slotted spoon. Pour the jelly into warm, clean jars and cover. Seal immediately.

Marmalades

ARMALADE is one of the most British of conventions – although it gets its name from the Portuguese for a quince, 'marmelo', the fruit from which this conserve was originally made. Marmalade was made famous by the Keiller family in the 18th century and it was they who first had the idea of including strips of rind in the orange jam or jelly. In the 1870s a Mrs. Cooper, a grocer's wife from Oxford, started making marmalade on a commercial scale, a business which took her name and is now synonymous with the best of British breakfasts. However, there are numerous delicious variations on the theme of orange marmalade to try out for yourself, as the following recipes demonstrate.

◆ EXTRA EQUIPMENT ◆

A food processor, with both coarse and fine cutters, is a great boon for making marmalade, although a meat grinder with a variety of blades does the job just as well, if not as quickly. A pressure cooker is also useful since citrus fruit rinds need to be softened thoroughly and require 1½–2 hours open boiling: a pressure cooker can cut this time down to between 10–20 minutes. (A warning note: do not fill your pressure cooker more than half full with fruit.)

◆ BASIC METHOD ◆

Using the basic equipment for jam-making, follow the instructions in the individual recipes and, for best marmalade results, observe the following tips:

★ Do not boil the shredded rind or peel too rapidly, because this will harden and toughen them.

★ The process of boiling with sugar is crucial – underboiled marmalade is too thin and will not keep well whereas, if overboiled, it stiffens and thickens like toffee. So keep the boil continuous and steady for 10–15 minutes, then boil fast to setting point.

★ Most of the pectin, so necessary for a good set, is in the pith and seeds of citrus fruits, rather than in the fruit pulp or juice, so these are important elements in the success of the marmalade-making process. They are usually tied up in a cheesecloth bag and cooked with the fruit in order to extract the pectin and bring it into solution. It is a good idea to tie the bag to the pan handle so that you can remove it more easily before adding the sugar.

★ Citrus fruits for marmalade should be just ripe. When using oranges, try to obtain Sevilles when they are in season because they have an exceptional flavor.

★ If the recipe says to peel the fruit, soak it first for a couple of minutes in boiling water, and it will peel off more easily.

★ Use a very sharp knife for shredding if you are not using a food mill or processor, and always cut smaller than you require in the end product since the rind swells slightly during cooking.

★ For a coarse-cut marmalade, you can boil the whole fruit for 2 hours first, and cut them in half and remove the seeds. Cut up the fruit, retaining as much juice as possible, and return the seeds to the water in which the fruit was first cooked. Boil for 5 minutes to extract the pectin, strain over the sliced fruit, add lemon juice and then continue the process of adding the sugar and cooking to setting point.

★ A jelly marmalade is made by boiling the shredded rind in a bag, keeping it separate from the main fruit mixture. This is then strained through a jelly bag and the liquid mixed with sugar and cooked to setting point with the addition of the shredded rind.

★ Always remove scum with a warm metal spoon as soon as setting point is reached. Leave the skimmed marmalade to cool until a thin skin begins to form on the surface, then stir gently to distribute the peel – if you do this, the peel will not rise to the top of the jar. If you are making jelly marmalades, however, leave them undisturbed.

★ Pack the marmalade into hot clean jars, leaving ½ inch head room. Wipe the jars carefully with a clean cloth. Wring out in boiling water, then adjust the lids and process in a boiling water bath (212°) for 10 minutes. Complete the seals if necessary and let cool. Wipe the jars clean with a damp cloth. Label attractively with the contents of the jar and the date. Store marmalade in a cool, dark, dry place.

PRESSURE COOKER METHOD

Put the cut or shredded rind or peel into the pressure cooker with the cheesecloth bag of seeds and pith. Add the water and cook at 10 lb pressure for 7–20 minutes (see table below). Open the cooker and remove the bag. Add the sugar and cook in the open cooker over a low heat until the sugar has dissolved. Bring to a boil and boil rapidly to setting point.

PRESSURE COOKER GUIDE

Cook at 10 lb pressure

GRAPEFRUIT	10 Minutes
LEMONS	7
LIMES	20
ORANGE JELLY MARMALADE	20
SEVILLE ORANGES	10
TANGERINES	12
ORANGES	7

Best Seville Marmalade

For all the hard work involved in making this marmalade, it is worth every minute – with its lovely deep brownish-orange color, and a taste quite incomparable with any purchased variety. So put aside a couple of days in January, when Seville oranges are in season, and you will be rewarded at breakfast time for the rest of the year!

5 lb Seville oranges
sugar

MAKES 10 lb

Wash and halve the oranges and squeeze the juice. Tie the seeds in a cheesecloth bag and soak them in 1¼ cups water for 30 minutes. Slice the orange rinds very finely.

Put the seed bag in a preserving kettle with the fruit. To every 1 lb fruit, add 2 quarts water. Add the juice and leave for 24 hours.

Simmer the fruit for about 2 hours until tender. Leave for a further 24 hours.

Measure the fruit into the cleaned preserving kettle. To every 1 lb fruit, add 3⅓ cups sugar. Stir over a gentle heat to dissolve the sugar. Bring to a boil and boil rapidly for about 10 minutes, stirring occasionally, or until setting point is reached.

Pack the marmalade into hot clean jars. Cover and process, then complete seals and cool.

Thick Quince Marmalade

*This is **the** original marmalade, historically speaking, because the name "marmalade" comes from the Portuguese **marmelo**, meaning a quince. A thick paste of quinces was an early medieval delicacy, an early form of marmalade which was later modified by the addition of citrus fruits, then later still made without any quinces at all. But if you can get hold of quinces, this is well worth making. It is a deep orange-red in color, thick in texture and quite individual in taste.*

quinces
sugar

Wash, remove the stalks and slice the quinces. Put into a preserving kettle and cover with water. Simmer gently for 40–50 minutes, stirring occasionally, until the fruit is very soft. Pass through a sieve to separate the pulp from the seeds.

Measure the pulp into the cleaned preserving kettle. To every 1 lb pulp, add 2 cups sugar. Stir over a medium heat until the sugar has dissolved. Simmer gently for about 10 minutes or until setting point is reached, stirring to prevent the quinces burning.

Pack the marmalade into hot clean jars. Cover and process, then complete seals and cool.

Fine-Cut Orange and Grapefruit Marmalade

The inclusion of grapefruit in marmalade is very refreshing – I love the fresh sharpness of this delicate marmalade. It is very simple and straightforward to make if you have a food processor to shred the rind. You can, of course, make this marmalade at any time of the year.

5 oranges	½ teaspoon baking soda
2 grapefruit	sugar
juice of 2 lemons	
5 pints water	MAKES 6 lb

Wash the fruit and cut in half. Squeeze the juice, reserving the pits. Slice the rinds very thinly. Alternatively shred them in a food processor. Tie the seeds in a cheesecloth bag.

Put the bag of seeds in a small saucepan with the lemon juice. Just cover with water and bring to a boil. Strain into a preserving kettle. Add the water, baking soda and shredded rind. Simmer, partially covered, for 1½ hours until the fruit is soft.

Measure the fruit and juice, for every 2½ cups add 2⅔ cups sugar. Stir over a medium heat until the sugar has dissolved. Bring to a boil and simmer for about 10 minutes, stirring occasionally, until setting point is reached.

Pack the marmalade into hot clean jars. Cover and process, then complete seals and cool.

Fine-Cut Green Tomato Marmalade

At the end of summer, when there are unripened tomatoes still on the vine with no hope of sun to turn them red, try making this delicate marmalade with its gingery flavor and exciting texture. Lovely on autumnal days, having tea in front of the first log fires of the colder weather.

6 lb green tomatoes	4½ lb (12 cups) sugar
rind and juice	1½ oz (1½-inches) fresh
of 2 lemons	ginger
	⅔ cup finely sliced
	candied peel

MAKES 8 lb

Stalk, wash and very finely slice the tomatoes. Put into a bowl with the lemon rind and juice. Cover with the sugar and leave for 24 hours.

Tie the fresh ginger in a cheesecloth bag. Put the tomato and sugar mixture into a preserving kettle with the ginger. Bring to a boil and simmer for about 30 minutes until tender.

When quite thick, remove the ginger and stir in the candied peel. Bring to a boil and boil rapidly for about 10 minutes, stirring occasionally, or until setting point is reached.

Pack the marmalade into hot clean jars. Cover and process, then complete seals and let cool.

Five Fruit Shred

This is a popular marmalade which you can make at any time of the year, a really useful standby on the pantry shelf. It also makes a perfect gift when attractively packed and labeled.

2 oranges	2 large pears
1 grapefruit	2 quarts water
1 lemon	3 lb (8 cups) sugar
2 large apples	

MAKES 5 lb

Wash and peel the citrus fruits. Cut off the pith. Shred the rind finely, either with a sharp knife or in a food processor. Chop the flesh coarsely and tie the pith and seeds in a cheesecloth bag.

Put the seed bag in a bowl with 1¼ cups of the water, the shredded rind, chopped fruit and remaining water. Soak for 24 hours.

Wash, peel and dice the apples and pears. Put the citrus fruit mixture into a preserving kettle with the apples and pears. Simmer for about 1¼ hours until well reduced, then remove the cheesecloth bag.

Add the sugar and stir over a gentle heat until dissolved. Bring to a boil and boil rapidly for about 10 minutes to setting point. Pack the marmalade into hot clean jars. Cover and process, then complete seals and let cool.

FIVE FRUIT SHRED (above)

Grapefruit and Pineapple Shred

These two fruits are the perfect foil for each other – a bittersweet combination which makes an unusual and original marmalade. I love to make this for Christmas time as something a little bit different.

2 large grapefruit	16-oz can crushed
2 lemons	pineapple, in natural
¼ teaspoon baking soda	juice
2 cups water	4 lb (10⅔ cups) sugar

MAKES 6 lb

Wash the grapefruit and lemons and remove the rind, cutting off and reserving the white pith. Very finely slice the rind with a sharp knife or in a food processor. Put the rind into a preserving kettle with the baking soda and water. Cover and simmer for 10 minutes. Drain.

Meanwhile, cut up the fruit pulp, keeping as much of the juices as possible. Tie the seeds and pith in a cheesecloth bag. Put the bag of seeds into the cleaned preserving kettle with the fruit pulp and pineapple. Cover and simmer for 15 minutes.

Add the softened rinds and the sugar. Stir over a gentle heat until the sugar has dissolved. Bring to a boil and boil rapidly for about 10 minutes, stirring occasionally, or until setting point is reached.

Pack the marmalade into hot clean jars. Cover and process, then complete seals and let cool.

Chunky Apricot and Lemon Marmalade

The individual, delicate taste of apricots makes a lovely marmalade combined with lemons; so when apricots are in plentiful supply in high summer, I often make this recipe.

1 lb apricots	2 quarts water
1 lb lemons	3 lb (8 cups) sugar

MAKES 5 lb

Wash, pit and coarsely chop the apricots. Wash and slice the lemons. Put apricots into a preserving kettle with the water and lemon slices. Leave to stand overnight.

Simmer for about 1 hour until very soft. Add the sugar and stir over a medium heat until dissolved. Bring to a boil and boil rapidly for about 10 minutes, stirring occasionally, or until setting point is reached.

Pack the marmalade into hot clean jars. Cover and process, then complete seals and let cool.

Chunky Melon Marmalade

Melon takes on a beautiful translucency and texture when it is cooked in syrup, and this lightly set, lemony marmalade adds a touch of style to any breakfast table.

1 lb lemons	3 lb (8 cups) sugar
⅔ cup water	1 cup liquid pectin
pinch of baking soda	
3 cups peeled, seeded and	MAKES 5 lb
diced melon, such as	
cantaloupe or	
honeydew	

Wash and peel the lemons. Halve and squeeze the juice. Remove the pith and slice the rind coarsely with a sharp knife or in a food processor.

Put the rind into a preserving kettle with the water, lemon juice and baking soda. Cover and simmer for 10 minutes. Add the melon and simmer for about 10 minutes until tender and transparent.

Add the sugar and stir over a gentle heat until dissolved. Bring to a boil and boil rapidly for 5 minutes. Remove from the heat and stir in the pectin.

Cool a little, skim if necessary and stir once again. Pack the marmalade into hot clean jars. Cover and process, then complete seals and let cool.

Lemon and Ginger Jelly Marmalade

There are not sufficient adjectives good enough for this marmalade! It is one of my greatest favorites because I love ginger and here, in combination with lemon jelly, it has a quite exquisite taste.

1½ lb lemons	2 lb (5⅓ cups) sugar
2 quarts water	1½ cups finely chopped
2 oz (2-inches) fresh	crystallized ginger
ginger	
	MAKES 5 lb

Wash and cut the lemons in quarters. Cut the pith off the rind and reserve it. Cut the rind into fine shreds with a sharp knife or in a food processor. Put the rind in a large bowl. Cut the fruit finely, reserving the seeds. Add the fruit to the bowl and cover with 1½ quarts of the water. Soak the seeds and pith separately in the remaining water for 6 hours.

Tie the fresh ginger in a cheesecloth bag. Strain the water from the seeds and pith into a preserving kettle and add the bag of ginger. Put in the fruit and rind with its soaking water. Bring to a boil, cover and simmer for 30–40 minutes. Remove the bag and strain the lemon mixture through a jelly bag for 2 hours.

Add the sugar and crystallized ginger. Stir over a low heat until the sugar has dissolved. Bring to a boil and boil rapidly for about 10 minutes, stirring occasionally, or until setting point is reached.

Pack the marmalade into hot clean jars. Cover and process, then complete seals and let cool.

Lime Marmalade

Now that fresh limes are so much more readily available, it makes sense to make one's own lime marmalade because the home-made variety is so much better than even the best brand name. The color of this marmalade is the loveliest of greens, an aristocrat among marmalades.

1 lb ripe limes	1½ lb (4 cups) sugar
3 cups water	
	MAKES 2–3 lb

Wash and thinly pare the limes. Very finely slice the rind. Halve the limes and squeeze the juice. Tie the seeds in a cheesecloth bag. Chop the rest of the pulp and tie in a separate cheesecloth bag.

Put the rind, juice, bag of seeds, bag of pulp and water into a preserving kettle. Bring to a boil and simmer for 1 hour.

Remove the bags. Add the sugar and stir over a gentle heat until dissolved. Bring to a boil and boil rapidly for about 10 minutes, stirring occasionally, or until setting point is reached.

Pack the marmalade into hot clean jars. Cover and process, then complete seals and let cool.

Tangerine Jelly Marmalade

I used to love tangerines as a child, and the name is so pretty, too! This member of the mandarin orange family is very common. If you prefer, you can substitute clementines (a cross between the tangerine and a standard orange) or other mandarins such as satsumas.

3 lb tangerines	5 lb (13⅓ cups) sugar
5 cups water	1 cup liquid pectin
juice of 3 lemons	
	MAKES 8 lb

Wash the tangerines. Put into a preserving kettle with the water. Cover and simmer for 20–25 minutes. Remove the fruit with a slotted spoon and leave to cool.

Skin the fruit and finely shred the rind. Reserve the seeds and coarse tissue and tie these in a cheesecloth bag. Add the bag to the liquid in the pan and boil hard for 5 minutes. Remove the bag of seeds and put the fruit and lemon juice into the pan. Simmer for 10 minutes. Strain through a jelly bag overnight.

Return the juice to the cleaned preserving kettle. Bring to a boil and boil for a few minutes. Add the sugar and stir over a low heat until dissolved. Add the slices and boil hard for 15 minutes. Remove from the heat and stir in the pectin.

Pack the marmalade into hot clean jars. Cover and process, then complete seals and let cool.

LIME MARMALADE (left) AND CHUNKY ORANGE HONEY MARMALADE (page 54)

Peach and Pineapple Marmalade

I had never used dried peaches in marmalade before I tried this recipe, and I was astonished at the result. It is almost like a Seville marmalade – lovely and sharp, a beautiful dark orange, with the occasional surprise of a chunk of pineapple to tease the palate.

2 lb (4⅔ cups) dried peaches	grated rind and juice of 2 lemons
1 lb can pineapple chunks	4 lb (10⅔ cups) sugar

MAKES 6 lb

Rinse and cover the dried peaches with warm water and soak overnight. Put into a preserving kettle with the soaking water. Simmer gently for about 20 minutes until tender.

Drain the pineapple chunks and cut each one in half. Remove the peaches from the pan with a slotted spoon, cool slightly, then roughly chop. Return to the pan with the lemon rind and juice, pineapple chunks and sugar. Stir over a gentle heat until the sugar has dissolved. Bring to a boil and boil rapidly for about 10 minutes, stirring occasionally, or until setting point is reached.

Pack the marmalade into hot clean jars. Cover and process, then complete seals and let cool.

Chunky Fig Marmalade

The combination of dried figs with ginger and lemon is exquisite, and provides a really gastronomic marmalade. As well as being delicious at breakfast time, it makes a very special addition to cream cheese and custards for desserts with a difference.

1 lb (3 cups) dried figs	⅓ cup chopped preserved ginger
½ lb (1⅓ cups) sugar	
grated rind and juice of 1 lemon	2 teaspoons ground ginger

MAKES 2 lb

Wash and chop the figs. Soak in water to cover overnight. Put the figs and soaking water into a preserving kettle and simmer for 10–15 minutes until tender.

Add the sugar and stir over a gentle heat until dissolved. Add the lemon rind and juice, preserved and ground ginger to the pan, stirring well. Bring to a boil and boil rapidly for about 10 minutes, stirring occasionally, or until setting point is reached.

Pack the marmalade into hot clean jars. Cover and process, then complete seals and let cool.

Tomato and Lemon Shred

This very unusual combination of ingredients makes a delicious marmalade with which I like to surprise guests when they come to stay. A distinguished addition to everyone's pantry shelf.

4 lb firm ripe tomatoes	3 lemons
4 oz (½ cup) crystallized ginger	3½ lb (9⅓ cups) sugar
	MAKES 5–6 lb

Pour boiling water over the tomatoes and skin them, then thinly slice. Cut the ginger into thin shreds. Wash and quarter the lemons, then cut into very thin slices. Tie the seeds in a cheesecloth bag.

Put the tomatoes into a preserving kettle with the lemon, bag of seeds, ginger and sugar. Add water to cover. Stand the pan over a very low heat on a heat diffuser to prevent burning. Stir until the sugar has dissolved.

Bring to a boil, then simmer very gently for up to 2 hours until thickened and setting point is reached.

Pack the marmalade into hot clean jars. Cover and process, then complete seals and let cool.

Dried Apricot and Ginger Marmalade

For anyone who loves apricots and ginger as much as I do, this is the perfect marmalade. The sharpness of the dried fruit is balanced by the sweet spiciness of the preserved ginger.

1 lb dried apricots	2 oz (2-inches) fresh ginger
2 quarts water	
4 oz (½ cup) preserved ginger	3 lb (8 cups) sugar
	MAKES 5 lb

Rinse and chop the apricots into small pieces. Put into a bowl, cover with the water and soak for 24 hours.

Cut the preserved ginger into tiny strips. Transfer the fruit to a preserving kettle and add the preserved ginger. Tie the fresh ginger in a cheesecloth bag and add to the pan. Bring slowly to a boil, then simmer for 40 minutes.

Add the sugar and stir over a low heat until dissolved. Bring to a boil and boil rapidly for about 10 minutes, stirring occasionally, or until setting point is reached. Remove the bag.

Pack the marmalade into hot clean jars. Cover and process, then complete seals and let cool.

Cherry Marmalade

This marmalade was made for England's Queen Henrietta Maria, as recorded by her Chancellor and friend, Sir Kenelme Digby in his book of 1669, "The Closet of Sir Kenelme Digby, Kt. Opened." Strictly speaking a marmalade is a jam made with citrus fruits, but this one qualifies as such because of its beautifully acidic quality, a sharpness which is gorgeous on breakfast toast, scones and crêpes.

½ lb (1⅔ cups) raspberries	2 lb (5⅓ cups) sugar juice of 1 lemon
3 lb (6 cups) cherries	
½ lb (2 cups) red currants	MAKES 4 lb

Hull and rinse the raspberries. Wash and pit the cherries. Rinse the red currants.

Put the raspberries and red currants into separate saucepans with water to cover. Bring each to a boil, cover and simmer for 10 minutes. Allow to cool in the pan. When cold, strain the juice and reserve.

Put the cherries into a preserving kettle with the fruit juices, sugar and lemon juice. Stir over a gentle heat until the sugar has dissolved. Bring to a boil and simmer for about 10 minutes, skimming occasionally, until setting point is reached.

Pack the marmalade into hot clean jars. Cover and process, then complete seals and let cool.

Chunky Orange Honey Marmalade

This unconventional marmalade is based on one from a very old edition of Mrs. Beeton, and is an interesting variation on the theme. The final marmalade is quite dry, rather like a paste of chunky peel sweetened with honey and softened in the cooking. It is well worth making for its individuality, but it has a short shelf life so it must be eaten within three weeks.

Seville oranges
clear honey

Wash and peel the oranges. Put the rinds into a preserving kettle with water to cover. Simmer for about 1½ hours until tender. Drain the rind, reserving the cooking liquid, and allow to cool.

Meanwhile, chop the fruit pulp and tie the seeds in a cheesecloth bag. Chop the cooled rinds. Add the rinds to the fruit pulp.

Measure the fruit into the cleaned preserving kettle. To every 1 lb fruit, add ¼ cup honey and 1¼ cups of the reserved cooking liquid. Add the bag of seeds and simmer for 30 minutes until reduced and thickened.

Pack the marmalade into hot clean jars and cover. Allow to cool completely before sealing (do not process).

Oxford Marmalade

This world-famous marmalade well deserves its reputation: its deep orange color is memorable and its uniquely strong flavor quite unforgettable. It is part and parcel of a good British breakfast!

3 lb Seville oranges   6 lb sugar
6 pints water

MAKES 10 lb

Wash and peel the oranges. Cut the peel into strips and the fruit into small pieces, reserving the pits. Put the pits into a small bowl. Put the strips of peel and chopped flesh into a large bowl. Bring the water to the boil and pour 1 pint over the pits and the remainder over the orange peel and flesh. Cover and leave for several hours or overnight.

Lift the pits out of the water with a slotted spoon and put them in a nylon sieve. Pour the water the pits were soaking in over the pits through the sieve into the large bowl. Repeat the process, using water from the large bowl. Discard the pits.

Boil the peel, flesh and water for about 2 hours or until the peel is very soft – the longer this mixture boils the darker the marmalade will be. When the peel is quite soft, remove the pan from the heat and add the sugar, stirring until it has dissolved. Boil very gently until the marmalade is as dark as you like it then boil rapidly for about 15 minutes to setting point. Take the pan off the heat and remove any scum with a slotted spoon. Leave to stand for 15 minutes, then stir to distribute the peel. Pot the marmalade in warm, clean jars. Cover and seal immediately.

Windfall Marmalade

The annual crop from the apple tree in my garden is often more than my family can eat fresh, so this recipe has become an established part of our autumn harvesting. It makes a marmalade with a difference – lemon and grapefruit peel in a sumptuous apple base.

2 lb windfall apples   5 pints water
2 grapefruit   5 lb sugar
4 lemons

MAKES ABOUT 9 lb

Peel, core and chop the apples, reserving the cores and peel. Wash and pare the rinds from the grapefruit and lemons as thinly as possible, using a sharp knife or potato peeler, and shred the rind finely. Remove the pith from the fruits and roughly chop the flesh, removing and reserving any pits. Tie the citrus pith, pits, apple peel and cores in a piece of cheesecloth. Put all the fruit in a preserving pan with the shredded rind, water and cheesecloth bag. Bring to the boil, then simmer gently for about 2½ hours until the peel is soft and the contents of the pan reduced by half.

Remove the cheesecloth bag, squeezing well and allowing the juice to run back into the pan. Add the sugar, stir until it has dissolved, then boil rapidly for 15–20 minutes to setting point. Take the pan off the heat and remove any scum with a slotted spoon. Let stand for 15 minutes, then stir to distribute the peel before potting into warm, clean jars. Cover and seal immediately.

Fruit Butters, Cheeses and Curds

FRUIT BUTTERS are an ideal way of using up fruit in a time of glut, and also of not wasting the fruit pulp left behind in the jelly bag after making jellies. When cooked to a stiff consistency, so they can be cut up into wedges, they are sometimes called fruit cheeses. They can be served as a dessert or as accompaniments to a wide variety of foods. Butters are of a softer consistency and are usually served as a spread as they contain less sugar and do not store for as long. Curds, which contain butter and eggs in addition to sugar and fruit, have a very short shelf life and are not made for storage. Refrigerate and eat as fresh as possible.

◆ SUITABLE FRUITS ◆

Gooseberries, cherries, black currants, quinces, plums, apples, apricots, crabapples, blackberries, raisins, lemons, oranges.

BASIC METHODS FOR BUTTER ◆ AND CHEESE MAKING ◆

Using the pulp left from making jellies

Remove the fruit pulp from the jelly bag and add enough water to process it to a purée in a blender. Sieve to separate the pulp from the seeds and skin. To every 2½ cups pulp, add 2⅔ cups sugar. Heat the mixture gently until the sugar has dissolved. Continue the cooking as below.

Using fresh fruit

Chop the fruit as necessary and put into a pan with water just to cover. Simmer until very tender. Sieve to separate the pulp from the seeds and skin. To every 1 lb pulp, add 2 cups sugar for fruit butters or 2⅔ cups sugar for fruit cheeses. Stir until the sugar has dissolved. Add the required spices if any, then simmer gently, stirring occasionally to prevent burning, until a thick, creamy consistency is reached (fruit butter), or (for fruit cheese) until a clean line is left when you draw a spoon across it. For long storage, pack into canning jars, leaving ½ inch headroom, and process in a boiling water bath as for jams and marmalades. Store in a cool, dark, dry place.

BASIC METHOD FOR CURD ◆ MAKING ◆

A curd is made rather like a fruit butter but with

the addition of eggs and butter. To prevent overheating and curdling, use a double boiler, or a bowl over a saucepan of simmering water, for this stage of the cooking. This lets the eggs heat to a solid set without separating and scrambling.

SERVING IDEAS FOR BUTTERS, CHEESES, AND CURDS

Fruit curds and butters can be served in much the same way as jellies. They go well with cold meats, with a bread and cheese lunch, and can be delicious folded into plain yogurt to flavor and sweeten it. They can be used like jams on bread, toast and scones, or in desserts that would normally use jams. You can serve fruit cheeses as a cold dessert in their own right, with custard sauce or cream, and they are a useful filling for sandwiches and tarts. Butters and curds add a delicious touch to crêpes and a wide variety of hot desserts.

STORING

Pack fruit butters into hot sterile canning jars. If not to be stored for long periods, fruit cheeses can be packed into buttered molds so that they are easy to turn out when required. While storing, cover with wax paper and an airtight top. Curds should be stored in clean jars with waxed discs and airtight covers. Store all these preserves in a cool, dark, dry place.

Orange Curd Special

This variation on a theme makes a surprisingly different curd from the lemon one. It is sweeter and less sharp in taste, and has the addition of candied orange peel which makes this curd utterly mouthwatering. Its glowing orange color looks gorgeous on the table, so with hungry folk around it never lasts for long.

4 tablespoons (½ stick) unsalted butter
2 oranges
1 lemon
⅓ cup finely chopped candied orange peel

½ lb (1⅓ cups) sugar
4 eggs

MAKES 1½ lb

Put the butter into a bowl and stand it in a pan of hot water until melted, or use a double boiler. Wash and finely grate the rinds of the oranges and lemon. Cut the fruit in half and squeeze the juice.

Stir the rinds, juice, candied peel and sugar into the butter and stir until the sugar has dissolved. Beat the eggs thoroughly and gradually add to the fruit mixture, stirring continuously. Simmer gently for 5–10 minutes, stirring, until the mixture thickens enough to coat the back of a wooden spoon.

Pack the curd into hot sterile jars. Cover and seal. Store in the refrigerator.

Lemon Curd

I love the way that the fresh sharpness of the lemon lifts the rich egg and butter mixture out of blandness, and the smooth thick texture of this curd is irresistible. Lemon curd has so many delicious uses – it is as good on fresh bread and scones as in pastry tarts, or as a filling for crêpes.

6 eggs
grated rind of 3 lemons
½ lb (2 sticks) unsalted butter

1 lb (2⅔ cups) sugar

MAKES 2 lb

Separate two of the eggs and set aside the whites to use for other purposes. Beat the four eggs and two extra yolks thoroughly. Squeeze the juices from two of the lemons.

Melt the butter in a bowl over a pan of boiling water, or in a double boiler, and stir in the sugar. When the sugar is warmed through, add the beaten eggs. Stir in the lemon rind and juice. Continue to stir for 5–10 minutes until the curd thickens, taking care that the mixture does not overheat or boil.

Pack the lemon curd in hot sterile jars. Cover and seal. When cold, store in the refrigerator.

ORANGE CURD SPECIAL (above left)

Elderberry Curd

To my mind the taste of elderberries is as good as that of black currants, and that is praise indeed for this most underestimated of wild fruits. In a good year, when elderberries are prolific and succulent, it is well worth making this recipe and serving it as an accompaniment to ice cream or sherbet. Or try folding the elderberry curd into yogurt to make a simple but memorable dessert.

1 lb (2 cups) elderberries	¾ lb (2 cups) sugar
8 tablespoons (1 stick) unsalted butter	4 eggs

MAKES 3 lb

Wash the berries. Put into a preserving kettle with a little water. Simmer for 10–15 minutes until soft. Sieve to separate the pulp from the seeds.

Put the purée into a bowl with the butter and sugar. Place the bowl over a pan of simmering water until the sugar has dissolved, stirring well. Alternatively, use a double boiler.

Beat the eggs, add to the fruit purée and stir over the hot water for 5–10 minutes until the mixture thickens.

Pack the curd into hot sterile jars. Cover and seal. Store in the refrigerator.

Plum and Raisin Spread

This interesting mixture of plums, oranges and raisins makes a thick and sumptuous spread for tea-time treats. With pretty labels and a fabric circle to cover the jar, it makes an original gift, too.

3 lb plums	3 lb (8 cups) sugar
2 oranges	1 lb (3 cups) seedless
2 cups water	raisins

MAKES 6 lb

Wash, halve and pit the plums. Wash, peel and finely slice the oranges. Put the plums into a preserving kettle with the water. Simmer for 10–15 minutes until tender and quite pulpy.

Sieve the plums and return to the cleaned preserving kettle with the orange slices, sugar and raisins. Stir over a low heat until the sugar has dissolved, then continue cooking for 5–10 minutes, stirring occasionally, until the mixture is thick.

Pack into hot clean jars. Cover and process, then complete seals and let cool.

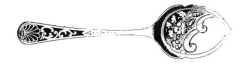

Pear Carnival Cheese

This brightly colored preserve deserves its carnival description – it is a mixture of red, green, orange and yellow, and full of appetizing tastes and textures. This cheese is one of the best preserves on freshly baked bread, and makes an unbeatable filling for an almond pastry case, served with whipped cream.

3 lb pears	sugar
16-oz can pineapple chunks, drained	⅔ cup canned cherries
grated rind and juice of 1 orange	MAKES 4 lb

Wash, peel and core the pears. Cut the flesh into ½-inch cubes. Add the pineapple and orange rind and juice.

Measure the fruits into a bowl. To every 1 lb fruit, add 2 cups sugar, sprinkling it over the fruits. Leave to stand overnight.

Transfer the mixture to a preserving kettle and simmer gently for 5–10 minutes, stirring frequently, until the mixture thickens. Cut the cherries in half and stir into the fruit.

Pack the cheese into hot clean jars. Cover and process, then complete seals and let cool. Store in a cool, dark place.

Raisin Cheese

This delectable cheese makes one of the most unexpectedly original additions to the pantry. It is a delicious variation on a kind of mincemeat theme: gorgeous in little light pastry cases or small patty shells, just warmed through, or as a filling for crêpes.

1 lb (3 cups) seedless raisins	2 teaspoons ground cloves
½ lb (1⅓ cups) sugar	⅔ cup chopped candied peel
2 teaspoons ground cinnamon	
	MAKES 2 lb

Put the raisins into a preserving kettle with water to cover, the sugar and spices. Simmer gently for 30 minutes, stirring continuously, until thick and stiff. Cool a little, then stir in the candied peel.

Pack the cheese into small, hot sterile jars (unless processing for long storage). Store in a dark, dry place.

Blackberry Cheese

Small wonder that hordes of people have eagerly gathered the blackberry harvest over the centuries. It is the finest and, happily, one of the most prolific of wild fruits, and has provided us with many classic pies and puddings, jams and jellies. This smooth, seedless cheese is a beautiful dark purplish-red in color, and is delicious served with plain yogurt or with ice cream.

2 lb (8 cups) blackberries   sugar
1¼ cups water

MAKES 3 lb

Rinse the blackberries. Put into a preserving kettle with the water. Cover and simmer for about 15–20 minutes until very soft. Rub the blackberries through a sieve. Return the pulp to the pan and continue cooking for 5–10 minutes to reduce the liquid content.

Measure the pulp into the cleaned preserving kettle. To every 2½ cups pulp, add 2⅔ cups sugar. Stir over a low heat until the sugar has dissolved. Simmer gently for 10–15 minutes until the mixture is thick.

Pack into small, hot, sterile jars. (Or pack into canning jars if processing.) Cover and seal.

Cherry Cheese

If you arm yourself with one of those great little gadgets, a pitter, which takes the pits out of small fruits cleanly and quickly, the time and effort taken to make this recipe will be greatly reduced. Ripe cherries are always a treat in high summer, so this is a luxury on the pantry shelf when they are long out of season.

cherries
sugar

Wash and pit the cherries, removing the stalks, working over a preserving kettle so that no juice is wasted, and using a pitter for this operation. Put into the preserving kettle with a little water and simmer very gently until the cherries are soft. Blend to a purée and then pass through a sieve to separate the pulp from the skins.

Measure the pulp into the cleaned preserving kettle. Bring to a boil and simmer for 5–10 minutes until a dry paste. To every 1 lb fruit, add 2⅔ cups sugar. Stir over a low heat until the sugar has dissolved, then stir continuously until a smooth, dry paste is obtained.

Pack into small buttered, sterile jars. Cover and seal. (Or pack into canning jars if processing.)

BLACKBERRY CHEESE (above left)

Cranberry Cheese

I love to serve this at Christmas instead of the traditional jelly, just for a change. It is thick and soft in texture, yet sharp and clean in taste, and takes a lot of beating as an accompaniment to roast turkey.

1½ lb cranberries, washed	1½ lb (3 cups) sugar
1½ pints water	MAKES ABOUT 2 lb

Put the cranberries in a saucepan with the water, bring to the boil then simmer gently for about 1 hour, or until the fruit is tender. Using a wooden spoon, press the fruit pulp through a nylon sieve. Return the purée to a clean pan, add the sugar and heat gently, stirring, until the sugar has dissolved. Bring to the boil and boil rapidly for about 30 minutes until the mixture is so thick the spoon leaves a clean line through it when drawn across the bottom of the pan.

Butter warm, clean jars with a little glycerine. Pot the cheese in the jars. Cover and seal.

Gooseberry Curd

All the curds are delicious, but for me there is something special about this one. The summery flavor of gooseberries in this creamy mixture makes it utterly delicious on toast or on freshly baked scones, and I also like to serve it rolled up in crêpes, with a little cream, as a dessert.

3 lb green gooseberries	4 oz (8 tablespoons) butter
450 ml (¾ pint) water	4 eggs, lightly beaten
1½ lb (3 cups) sugar	
	MAKES 4 lb

Top, tail and wash the gooseberries. Put them with the water in a saucepan and simmer gently for 20 minutes, or until tender. Using a wooden spoon, press the gooseberry pulp through a nylon sieve into the top of a double boiler or a bowl standing over a pan of simmering water. Add the sugar, butter and eggs. Heat gently, stirring, for about 20 minutes until the sugar has dissolved and the mixture thickens, taking care that the mixture does not overheat or boil.

Strain, then pot in small, warm, clean jars. Cover and seal. When cold, store in the refrigerator.

Crunchy Harvest Butter

A delectable hint of walnuts highlights both the flavor and the texture of the apple purée that forms the basis of this recipe. The added crunch of natural wheat germ is quite unusual, and if you choose to make the butter with crab apples their slightly sharper taste combines particularly well with the overall nutty taste.

3 lb cooking apples or, crab apples	½ cup walnuts, finely chopped
about 1¾ pints water sugar	3 tablespoons wheat germ
	MAKES 3 lb

Wash and chop the apples. Put into a saucepan, cover with water, bring to the boil and simmer gently for about 1 hour until really soft and pulpy. Using a wooden spoon, press the apple pulp through a nylon sieve and measure the purée. Return the purée to the pan and add 12 oz (1½ cups) sugar for each 20 oz purée. Heat gently, stirring, until the sugar has dissolved, then bring to the boil and boil for 30–45 minutes, stirring frequently, until the mixture is thick and like jam in consistency. Stir in the walnuts and wheat germ. Pot the butter in warm, clean jars and cover with airtight tops. Immerse in a pan of hot water and boil for 5 minutes. Remove the jars from the water and cool. Store in a dark, dry, cool place.

Apricot and Orange Butter

The two fruity flavors of apricot and orange are beautifully balanced in this recipe, and complement each other perfectly. It makes a delicious accompaniment to roast chicken, as well as being irresistible on fresh toast.

3 lb fresh apricots grated rind and juice of 2 oranges	about 2 cups water sugar
	MAKES ABOUT 3 lb

Skin and pit the apricots. Put them with the orange rind and juice in a pan and add just enough water to cover. Simmer gently for about 45 minutes until the fruit is soft and pulpy. Press the fruit through a sieve. Measure the purée and return it to the pan with 12 oz (1½ cups) sugar for each 20 oz purée. Heat gently, stirring, until the sugar has dissolved, then bring to the boil and boil for 30–40 minutes, stirring frequently, until the mixture is thick and like jam in consistency. Pot the butter in warm, clean jars and cover with airtight tops. Immerse in a pan of hot water and boil for 5 minutes. Remove the jars from the water and cool. Store in a dark, dry, cool place.

Crab Apple Butter

This is based on traditional country recipe of the 18th century – a time when the homemaker made the most of the wild harvest every autumn, and when these fruits were cherished for their food value as well as their delicious flavors. This spicy butter goes particularly well with roast meat or chicken, either hot or as part of a cold table.

3 lb crab apples	2-inch stick cinnamon
2½ cups hard cider	½ teaspoon cloves
2½ cups water	
sugar	MAKES 5 lb

Wash and cut the crab apples into quarters. Put in a preserving kettle with the cider and water. Simmer for 15–20 minutes until soft and pulpy. Press the fruit through a sieve.

Measure the pulp into the cleaned preserving kettle. To every 1 lb pulp, add 2 cups sugar. Stir over a low heat until the sugar has dissolved. Tie the spices in a cheesecloth bag and add to the pan. Bring to a boil, stirring frequently, and simmer for 5–10 minutes until the mixture is a thick, creamy consistency.

Pack the butter into hot clean jars and cover. Process, complete the seals and let cool. Store in a dark, dry, cool place.

Plum Butter

This way of using damson plums is one of the most delightful, as their sharp and distinctive flavor is an excellent foil for the smooth, slightly spiced butter. Other plums such as beach and greengage may be used instead of damsons.

damson plums	sugar
whole blanched almonds	ground allspice to taste

Wash and pick the stalks off the plums. Chop a few almonds. Put the plums into a preserving kettle with a little water. Simmer for 10–15 minutes until soft, stirring occasionally. Press the plums through a coarse sieve.

Measure the sieved fruit into the cleaned preserving kettle. To every 1 lb pulp, add 2 cups sugar. Stir over a gentle heat until the sugar has dissolved. Add the allspice to taste and the chopped almonds. Simmer gently for 5–10 minutes until the mixture is a smooth, buttery consistency.

Pack the butter into hot clean jars and cover. Process, then complete the seals and let cool. Store in a dark, dry, cool place.

Special Conserves

CONSERVES have a special quality all their own – a touch of luxury, of originality, to which can be added their good looks. The way that the whole fruits are preserved in syrup makes the jars, glistening with seductive goodies, look really mouthwatering. It is worth saving extra-large jars for this operation, or even buying them especially, to show the conserves off to their best advantage. It is well worth experimenting with the wide range of tropical fruits that are available to add an extravagant touch to the pantry shelf.

BEST FRUITS FOR MAKING CONSERVES

Since conserves are made rather as luxury items, it is best to choose fruits that are going to look good in the jars: all the soft summer fruits lend themselves well to conserves – strawberries, raspberries, gooseberries, black currants, red and white currants, cranberries – and, later on in the year, blackberries. Tiny kumquats look gorgeous preserved whole, so do chunks of pineapple and quartered nectarines. Apricots, whether dried or fresh, take on a golden glow when preserved in syrup, and make some of the very best conserves.

STORING

These special conserves are not made for long storage, although they should be processed in a boiling water bath (212°) for 10 minutes. The only preservatives they contain are sugar and a little alcohol or vinegar, so their shelf life is fairly short. It is best to eat them within six weeks. Keep conserves in as cool a place as possible – if you have room to keep them in the refrigerator, they will keep for slightly longer.

NOTES ON STERILIZING JARS

Some people like to sterilize their jars before filling them with preserves, although this shouldn't be necessary if the preserve is to be processed in a boiling water bath. All jars (and lids) should be washed in hot soapy water and rinsed well in scalding water. Keep filled or covered with hot water until used. To sterilize, stand the open jars in a large kettle, add hot water to submerge the jars and bring to a boil. Boil for 15 minutes.

JARS

Choose canning jars in prime condition for storing conserves. However, if you are making them as gifts you may feel moved to go so far as to buy special ones. There is a variety to choose from, with details like fluting, faceting and beading, and some made with tinted glass. When you fill the jars with your luscious conserves and package them up as gifts, these make extra special presents, homemade with style.

➤ MAKING UP GIFT JARS ➤

One of the prettiest ways of converting a plain glass jar into an attractive looking gift is to cut out a circle of printed fabric 1 inch larger in diameter than the top of the jar. Cut it using pinking shears if you can, to give the edge a zig-zag pattern and also to stop it from fraying. Place the fabric circle evenly over the top of the sealed jar, and tie it down with fine cord or very thin ribbon, making a secure knot first and then tying it into a bow.

There are a number of very pretty self-adhesive labels for preserves on the market nowadays, so it is worth hunting around for ones that will look good with the type of fabric you have chosen. Neatly write, in colored pen to match your color scheme, the name of the preserve, with the date on which it was made. Stick the label on, and you have an attractive gift to give away.

Spiced Green Figs

To my mind, ripe figs are among the most sensual of summer fruits, and their richness and soft texture lend themselves beautifully to spicing with cinnamon and cloves. Serve these figs as part of a cold table – they are really delicious with cheeses, salads, and cold cuts of all kinds.

4 lb ripe figs	2½ cups vinegar
2 quarts strong brine (see page 85)	½ oz cinnamon sticks (about 8–10)
2 lb (5⅓ cups) sugar	2 tablespoons whole cloves

MAKES 7 lb

Wipe the figs. Put into a bowl and pour over the brine. Leave to soak overnight.

Put the sugar and vinegar in a heavy pan. Stir over a gentle heat until the sugar has dissolved. Tie the spices in a cheesecloth bag and add to the pan. Bring to a boil and simmer for 5 minutes. Remove the spices and boil the vinegar hard for about 5 minutes to reduce.

Rinse the figs thoroughly in cold water and dry well. Pack into hot clean jars.

Pour the boiling vinegar over the figs. Cover and process, then complete the seal and let cool.

Spiced Gooseberries

Gooseberries lend themselves beautifully to preserving, and this spicy conserve makes a lovely addition to a bread and cheese lunch or a salad buffet table. Excellent with coleslaw, too.

6 lb (16 cups) gooseberries	2 teaspoons ground allspice
4 lb (10⅔ cups) sugar	1 teaspoon ground cloves
1¼ cups malt vinegar	
2 teaspoons ground cinnamon	MAKES 8 lb

Top, tail and wash the gooseberries. Drain and dry them thoroughly.

Place the gooseberries in large sterile jars or dishes and sprinkle over the sugar. Warm in preheated 325° oven for 1 hour.

Transfer the sweetened gooseberries to an aluminum preserving kettle. Stir in the vinegar and spices. Bring to a boil and boil for about 20–30 minutes until very thick.

Pack the conserve into hot clean jars. Cover and process, then complete the seals and let cool.

Spiced Blackberries

Since most blackberry recipes are for sweet preserves, it is rather nice to try a savory one for a change. These spiced blackberries keep indefinitely and I love to take them on summer picnics or to serve them with a cheese and salad meal. The blackberries retain all their distinctive and delicate flavor, and are excellent just with plain bread and cheese.

2 lb (8 cups) blackberries	1 teaspoon whole cloves
1 lb (2⅔ cups) sugar	1 teaspoon ground ginger
1¼ cups vinegar	
1 teaspoon allspice berries	MAKES 3 lb

Wash and pick over the blackberries. Put the sugar in an aluminum preserving kettle with the vinegar and stir over a gentle heat until dissolved.

Put the whole spices in a cheesecloth bag and add to the pan. Simmer for several minutes. Add the blackberries and ginger and poach gently for 10–15 minutes. Remove the bag of spices.

Pack the blackberries into hot clean jars. Boil the vinegar hard until it turns syrupy. Pour the vinegar over the blackberries. Cover and process, then complete the seals and let cool.

Brandied Apricots

*I love to make jars of these as little presents –
the golden glow of apricots set in a glistening
syrup, which is laced with brandy, looks and
tastes quite epicurean. Attractively labeled, and
with a circle of printed fabric over the top of the
jar, they make personal and original gifts.*

2 lb fresh apricots	1¼ cups brandy
½ lb (1⅓ cups) sugar	
	MAKES 2 lb

Wipe the apricots and remove the pits as carefully as
possible without injuring the fruit. Put into a large
Mason container, such as a kilner jar, sprinkling
with the sugar as you fill. Pour the brandy over the
fruit and tightly cover the jar.

Place the jar in a pan of simmering water and
bring the brandy to simmering, but do not allow it to
boil. Heat at this point for 15–20 minutes.

Carefully remove the fruit with a slotted spoon
and pack into small, hot sterile jars. Pour over the
sweetened brandy. Leave until cold. Cover and seal.

Brandy Berries

*I came across this delectable conserve when I
visited my aunt some time ago and it has
remained in my memory as being quite
outstandingly delicious. Cherries, plums or
peaches can be used instead of cranberries. This
conserve is, of course, a luxury because of its
liberal use of alcohol but well worth treating
yourself to!*

1 lb (3 cups) fresh cranberries	⅔ cup Grand Marnier and brandy mixed
1 lb (2⅔ cups) sugar	
grated rind of 1 orange	MAKES 2 lb

Wash and dry the cranberries and pick them over.
Put the cranberries, sugar, orange rind and liqueur
and brandy in a large, flat, ovenproof dish and leave
to stand for 30 minutes.

Cover the dish with foil and cook in a preheated
325° for 30 minutes. Cool slightly.

Pack the conserve into hot sterile jars. Cover and
seal. Store in a cool place.

BRANDY BERRIES (above)

Holiday Conserve

This luxury mixture of apricots, glacé fruits and nuts, flavored with orange and lemon, is a real treat which I like to have on hand when it is holiday time. Served with homemade ice cream and brandy snaps, we never fail to feel festive!

1 lb canned apricots halves	¼ teaspoon grated nutmeg
½ lb (1½–2 cups) mixed glacé fruits	grated rind of 1 orange
⅔ cup glacé cherries	grated rind of 1 lemon
½ lb (1⅓ cups) sugar	3 cups finely chopped Brazil nuts or walnuts (12 oz)
¼ teaspoon salt	

MAKES 3 lb

Drain the apricots, reserving the syrup, and coarsely chop. Add enough water to the syrup to yield 2 cups.

Place all the ingredients, except the nuts, in a preserving kettle. Bring to a boil, stirring occasionally, and simmer for 25 minutes until thickened.

Stir the nuts into the conserve for the last 5 minutes of cooking.

Pack the conserve into hot clean jars. Cover and process, then complete the seals and let cool.

Orange Cranberry Conserve

It has become far easier to buy fresh cranberries in recent years, and this orange-flavored mixture with raisins and nuts makes a specialty conserve. As well as a treat to have in store, it also makes a lovely gift – a present with a difference.

1 lb (3 cups) cranberries	⅓ cup raisins
2 oranges	⅓ cup walnuts
1¼ cups water	¾ lb (2 cups) sugar

MAKES 2 lb

Wash and pick over the cranberries. Wash, peel and finely slice the oranges, discarding the pits. Cut the slices into quarters.

Put the fruit into a preserving kettle with the water. Simmer for about 15–20 minutes until tender.

Add the raisins, walnuts and sugar. Stir over a gentle heat until the sugar has dissolved. Bring to a boil and boil rapidly for about 10 minutes, stirring occasionally, or until setting point is reached.

Pack the conserve into hot clean jars. Cover and process, then complete the seals and let cool.

Preserved Nectarines

I made these as Christmas presents one year and they made a real impact – the friends who received them all wanted the recipe and so here, in all its simplicity, it is.

1 lb nectarines	⅔ cup peach brandy
1 lb (2⅔ cups) sugar	
⅔ cup water	MAKES 2 lb

Wash, halve and pit the nectarines. Put the sugar into a preserving kettle with the water and stir over a gentle heat until dissolved. Bring to a boil and boil for 10 minutes to make a syrup.

Place the nectarines in the hot syrup and poach, just below simmering point, for 5 minutes. Leave to cool in the syrup.

Lift out the fruit with a slotted spoon and put into hot clean jars. Reheat the syrup and boil hard for 5 minutes. Cool a little and stir in the brandy.

Pour the brandy syrup over the nectarines. Cover and process, then complete the seals and let cool. Store in a cool, dry place.

Pear and Pineapple Conserve

The combination of these two fruits, glistening in syrup and slightly translucent, is quite lovely – and it tastes as delicious as it looks. This conserve is fabulous with a sharp-tasting citrus sherbet and ice cream, especially coffee-flavored.

2 lb (5⅓ cups) sugar	2 lb pears
2½ cups water	1 large pineapple
	MAKES 5 lb

Put the sugar into a preserving kettle with the water and stir until dissolved. Bring to a boil and simmer for 10 minutes until a fairly thick syrup.

Wash, peel and core the pears, then slice into eight segments each. Remove the skin from the pineapple and cut the flesh into thick slices. Chop each slice into eight triangles.

Place the pineapple pieces in the syrup and poach for 30 minutes, then add the pears for the last 10 minutes of the cooking time.

Lift out the fruit and put into hot clean jars. Pour over the syrup. Cover and process, then complete the seals and let cool. Store in a cool, dry place.

Orange Mincemeat

This is my very favorite mincemeat recipe, so fruity and fresh, instead of the rather heavy, solid mincemeats that abound. It is good enough to eat out of the jar, but if you can resist doing that, try filling little pastry cases with the mincemeat and heating them through gently – they are quite scrumptious.

2 oranges	¾ cup ground almonds
2 lemons	½ lb (1⅓ cups) chopped
1 lb apples	candied peel
1 lb (2⅔ cups) currants	1⅓ cups light brown
1 lb (2⅔ cups) raisins	sugar
½ lb (1⅓ cups) golden	⅔ cup brandy
raisins	
½ lb (2 cups) unskinned	MAKES 6 lb
whole almonds	

Wash and pare the rind off the oranges and lemons and shred them finely. Simmer the shredded rind in a saucepan of boiling water for 10 minutes. Drain and cool. Squeeze the juice from the oranges and lemons. Wash, peel, core and chop the apples.

Mix the apples, currants, raisins and golden raisins with the fruit juices and put small amounts at a time through a food processor just to break them up a little.

Coarsely chop the whole almonds. Stir the rinds, ground almonds, candied peel, sugar, almonds and brandy into the apple mixture and mix thoroughly.

Pack the mincemeat into hot sterile jars. Cover and seal. Store in a cook, dark, dry place for up to 3 months.

Strawberries in Wine

This is a summer treat with a difference which I love to make when the strawberry season is at its height and I have enough jam on the shelf. Served with a sherbet or ice cream, these strawberries in their delicious wine syrup make a fantastic finale to a meal.

strawberries
sugar
sherry or Madeira

Hull, rinse and dry the strawberries. Weigh the strawberries. To every 3 cups fruit, use ⅔ cup sugar.

Put the strawberries into sterile jars, sprinkling with the sugar as you fill. When the fruit reaches the neck of the jar, fill it up with sherry or Madeira.

Cover and seal tightly. Store in a cold place, preferably the refrigerator.

STRAWBERRIES IN WINE (above)

Chutneys

WIDE variety of fruit and vegetables can be used to make chutneys. Traditionally, apples and onions provide the basis, with raisins and dates often to be found on the ingredients list. Plums, squash, gooseberries and tomatoes also make lovely chutneys, and shallots and garlic are often added to give them zest and flavor. Chutneys are frequently laced with hot spices such as chilies, peppercorns and mustard seeds to provide a hot tang.

While most fruit and vegetables are boiled to produce a thick mixture, there is a range of chutneys which are uncooked, and are served rather like condiments to spice up a meal.

BASIC METHOD

Use fresh fruit or vegetables which are not over-ripe or damaged. Prepare them and put into an aluminum pan (metals such as brass, copper or iron will react with the acid in the vinegar and spoil both the chutney and the pan). If you choose to use a pressure cooker, never fill it more than half full and, generally speaking, cook at 15 lb pressure for 10 minutes. When cooking in an open preserving kettle, long steady cooking is required for a good chutney, but do not over-boil

it. As soon as the mixture thickens to the point where pools of vinegar no longer collect on the surface, the chutney is ready. If sieving is called for, use a nylon sieve, since a metal one will impart an unpleasant taste.

Pack the hot chutney into hot, clean canning jars, leaving ½-inch headroom. Remove any trapped air by running the blade of a table knife down the inside of the jar several times. Cover and process in a boiling water bath (212°) to ensure sterilization and a good seal, then complete the seals if necessary. Wipe the jars clean with a damp cloth, then label. Store in a cool, dark, dry place. Some chutneys keep for many years, even up to twenty, and improve greatly with keeping.

HOW TO SERVE

Serve chutneys with hot meals like curries, rice dishes, stews and casseroles. They make a pleasant change to eat with roast chicken or lamb, and certain ones are excellent with fish dishes. Try mixing small amounts of chutney into stuffings to spice them up and sharpen the flavor. A selection of chutneys greatly enhances a cold table – they are excellent with salads and cold cuts.

Mango Chutney

The classic accompaniment to an Indian meal of curries and rice, this sweet chutney, with its mouthwatering texture, is well worth making. I love mango chutney with cheese, too, especially a strong blue Stilton or Gorgonzola. With some fresh bread, it makes a perfect meal.

2 lb mangoes	2½ cups vinegar
3 oz (¼ cup) salt	1 lb (2⅔ cups) sugar
1 lb tart apples	½ teaspoon grated
1 medium onion	nutmeg
2 limes	½ teaspoon ground
3 oz (3-inches) fresh	cinnamon
ginger root	⅔ cup raisins

MAKES 4 lb

Peel and finely slice the mangoes. Put them into a bowl and sprinkle with the salt. Wash, core and chop the apples. Skin and slice the onion. Wash and slice the limes. Bruise the ginger and tie in a cheesecloth bag.

Put half of the vinegar into an aluminum preserving kettle with the sugar and stir over a medium heat until dissolved. Bring to a boil and boil for 5–8 minutes to make a syrup.

Add the rest of the vinegar, the mangoes, spices and onion. Simmer for 10 minutes. Add the remaining ingredients and simmer for a further 40–50 minutes until thick.

Pack into hot clean jars, cover and process, then let cool.

Fig and Nut Chutney

Rich and thick, this exciting combination of fresh figs, dates and nuts makes an exquisite and piquant side dish to accompany plain roast chicken. It is also delicious with lightly spiced rice and a tomato and onion salad.

1½ lb fresh figs	2½ oz (⅓ cup) chopped
½ lb onions	preserved ginger
½ lb (1⅓ cups) brown	1 cup chopped hazelnuts
sugar	½ cup chopped raisins
2½ cups vinegar	½ teaspoon salt
½ cup chopped dates	¼ teaspoon cayenne

MAKES 5 lb

Wipe and slice the figs. Skin and slice the onions. Put the sugar in an aluminum preserving kettle with the vinegar and stir over a medium heat until dissolved. Bring to a boil and simmer for 10 minutes.

Put the other ingredients into a large bowl and pour over the sweetened vinegar. Leave to stand overnight.

Return the mixture to the pan and bring slowly to a boil. Simmer for 1–2 hours until dark and thick.

Pack into hot clean jars, cover and process, the let cool.

Carrot Chutney

This rather dry, slightly sweet chutney is very versatile. I love to serve it with salads of all kinds at any time of the year. Carrot chutney makes a delicious addition to stuffings, making them a little different. It goes beautifully with cream cheese and cottage cheese, too, adding texture and spice to their blandness.

5⅓ cups grated carrots	2 teaspoons apple pie
1 cup brown sugar	spice
⅔ cup golden raisins	12 peppercorns
3¾ cup vinegar	2 bay leaves
2 teaspoons ground ginger	MAKES 3 lb

Put into an aluminum preserving kettle with all the other ingredients. Simmer for about 10 minutes until tender, thickened and the liquid has evaporated.

Pack into hot clean jars, cover and process, let cool.

Apricot and Raisin Chutney

Sweet chutneys provide a delicious finishing touch to cold cuts, cheeses and salads. This slightly hot, spicy way of dealing with dried apricots and raisins is an original and ever popular addition to cold, simple fare.

1½ lb dried apricots	1¼ cups vinegar
1 quart hot water	1 lb (2⅔ cups) sugar
10 large garlic cloves	¼ teaspoon salt
3-inch piece of fresh ginger	¼ teaspoon cayenne
	1 cup golden raisins
	MAKES 5 lb

Rinse and put the apricots in a bowl with the hot water. Leave to soak for 4 hours.

Chop the garlic. Peel and chop the ginger. Blend the garlic and ginger with a little of the vinegar until smooth. Put the apricots with their soaking water and the ginger and garlic mixture into an aluminum preserving kettle with the rest of the vinegar. Add the sugar, salt and cayenne. Bring to a boil and simmer gently for 45 minutes, stirring occasionally to prevent burning.

Add the raisins and continue cooking until the chutney thickens and begins to turn shiny.

Pack into hot clean jars, cover, process and cool.

APRICOT AND RAISIN CHUTNEY (above)

Grapefruit Chutney

*This is one of my firm favorites, because of the
lovely sharp flavor of grapefruit and the
unexpected crunch of almonds. It is
fabulous with an eggplant curry and basmati
rice, and is a delicious accompaniment to an
avocado and raw mushroom salad.*

2 lb (4 cups) grapefruit pulp	2½ cups vinegar
1½ lb (4 cups) sugar	⅔ cup raisins
1 teaspoon ground cloves	⅔ cup golden raisins
1 teaspoon cayenne	12 blanched almonds

Discard the seeds and pith from the grapefruit pulp.
Put the pulp into an aluminum preserving kettle
with the sugar.

Stir over a gentle heat until the sugar has
dissolved. Stir in the ground spices, vinegar and
raisins. Bring to a boil and simmer gently until soft
and thick. Chop the almonds and stir into the
chutney toward the end of the cooking time.

Pack into hot clean jars, cover and process, then
let cool.

Eggplant Chutney

*This recipe comes from India where the word
chutney originates – chatni, a Hindi word,
means a relish of sweet fruits or vegetables with
vinegar and spices. Serve this one with a meat
or vegetable curry and rice, and it really comes
into its own.*

2 lb eggplants	2 teaspoons ground ginger
3 medium onions	1 teaspoon salt
1 lb tart apples	1¼ lb (3⅓ cups) dark brown sugar
2 teaspoons pickling spices	
1¼ cups vinegar	

MAKES 5 lb

Peel and cut the eggplants into long segments, then
into thickish slices. Skin and very finely chop the
onions. Wash, core and roughly chop the apples. Tie
the pickling spices in a cheesecloth bag.

Put all the ingredients, except the sugar, into an
aluminum preserving kettle and simmer for
30–40 minutes until tender. Remove the spice bag
and add the sugar. Stir over a gentle heat until the
sugar has dissolved. Simmer until the chutney
becomes thick and lustrous.

Pack into hot clean jars, cover and process, then
let cool.

Autumn Chutney

There is nothing quite like the satisfaction to be gained from using up surplus vegetables and fruits at the end of the summer as the evenings close in a little and the air begins to chill. The smell of this lovely mixed chutney always reminds me of those golden, slightly misty days as we prepare for winter.

1 lb plums
1 lb apples
1 lb tomatoes
4 medium onions
2 large garlic cloves
1 lb (3 cups) golden
   raisins
2½ cups vinegar

¼ teaspoon ground mace
¼ teaspoon apple pie
   spice
2 tablespoons ground
   ginger
2⅔ cups light brown
   sugar

MAKES 7 lb

Wash, halve and pit the plums. Peel and core the apples. Wash and chop the tomatoes. Skin and slice the onions. Skin and chop the garlic.

Mix the fruit and vegetables together and put into an aluminum preserving kettle with all the other ingredients, except the sugar. Simmer for about 30 minutes until tender.

Add the sugar and stir until dissolved. Simmer gently, stirring frequently, until thick.

Pack into hot clean jars, cover and process, then let cool.

Bengal Chutney

A hot chutney to raise the roof of the mouth! Not for timid tastebuds this one, but for chili-lovers for whom a hot chutney maks a complete meal of a vindaloo! Keep for 2–3 years before using – it improves greatly with keeping, and the longer the better.

15 large tart apples	2⅔ cups light brown
½ lb onions	sugar
20 garlic cloves	3¾ cups vinegar
2 fresh chilies	⅓ cup mustard seeds
1⅓ cups raisins	½ cup ground ginger

MAKES 8 lb

Wash the apples and bake in a preheated 350° oven for 20–30 minutes until soft. Scoop out the flesh from the skins and remove the seeds.

Skin and chop the onions and put into a pan of boiling water with the garlic. Simmer for about 20 minutes until soft.

Wash and slice the chilies. Put the onion and apple pulp into a preserving kettle with all the other ingredients. Bring to a boil and simmer for 15–20 minutes.

Pack the chutney into hot clean jars. Cover and process, then let cool.

Banana and Lychee Chutney

The texture of lychees gives a mouthwatering crunch to this unusual chutney. The flavor of banana provides a distinctive taste, and it makes an elegant companion to a dish of cold chicken.

12 lychees	1⅓ cups raisins
1 large banana	4 teaspoons salt
2 medium onions	1 teaspoon ground ginger
2 lemons	½ teaspoon pepper
⅔ cups sliced preserved	1¼ cups vinegar
ginger	

MAKES 2 lb

Peel and chop the lychees. Peel and slice the banana. Skin and grate the onions. Peel and cut the lemons into small chunks.

Put all the ingredients into an aluminum preserving kettle and simmer for about 1½ hours. Mash to a rough purée with a plastic-coated masher.

Pack into hot clean jars, cover, process and let cool.

BANANA AND LYCHEE CHUTNEY (above)

Apple, Banana and Apricot Chutney

A slight suggestion of curry gives this sweet fruit chutney bite and zest. It is delicious in cheese sandwiches, and a great favorite on a picnic with children, who always seem to love the banana flavor which comes through so strongly.

⅔ cup dried apricots	1 teaspoon ground ginger
2 lb tart apples	¼ cup curry powder
6 bananas	1⅓ cups dark brown
3 medium onions	sugar
¼ lb (⅓ cup) salt	2½ cups vinegar
1 teaspoon ground	
cinnamon	MAKES 4 lb

Rinse the apricots, cover with water and soak overnight. Wash, peel, core and slice the apples. Drain and chop the apricots. Peel and slice the bananas and onions.

Put all the ingredients into an aluminum preserving kettle. Bring to a boil and simmer very gently for 1–1½ hours, stirring frequently, until thick.

Pack into hot clean jars, cover and process, then let cool.

Date and Plum Chutney

Rich and spicy, this chutney is deliciously different and takes its place with style on a cold buffet table. It goes particularly well with salamis and pâtés, so comes into its own in the summer months for salad meals.

3 lb plums	½ teaspoon ground
¾ lb dates	ginger
3 small onions	½ teaspoon ground black
2½ cups malt vinegar	pepper
1½ lb (4 cups) sugar	1 teaspoon grated nutmeg
1 tablespoon salt	
	MAKES 6 lb

Wipe, halve and pit the plums. Pit and chop the dates. Skin and finely slice the onions.

Put the plums in an aluminum preserving kettle with the vinegar, dates and onions. Simmer for 15–20 minutes until soft.

Stir in the sugar, salt and spices. Simmer until the mixture thickens, stirring frequently to prevent burning.

Pack into hot clean jars, cover and process, then let cool.

Pickles and Relishes

THE addition of pickles and relishes to salad meals, buffet parties, and even the simplest of Cheese sandwich lunches provides a delicious finishing touch. Their sharp tastes, often strong ones, go beautifully with rich foods like curries, or with simple egg and cheese dishes, for example. Unusual ingredients such as watermelon rind and green walnuts come into their own in this department, and when there is a glut of summer vegetables this is a great way of dealing with them so that you can enjoy them later.

SUITABLE FRUIT AND VEGETABLES

A wide variety of fruits, vegetables, herbs and spices are used in pickles and relishes, ranging from cauliflowers, shallots, kidney beans, apples, onions, artichokes and beets, to lemons, melons, peaches and pears. Gherkins and red cabbage are delicious pickled, as are mushrooms, along with less usual ingredients like walnuts, nasturtium seeds and watermelon rind. The art of making good pickles is to establish the right balance between sourness, saltiness and sweetness: you can make any of these predominate by adjusting the quantities of vinegar, salt and sugar.

BRINING TECHNIQUES

Brine is a solution of salt and water that is usually measured by percentage. A 10% brine is normally used when making vegetable pickles and relishes, and this requires ½ cup salt to every 5 cups water. When vinegar is used in the preserving process, the percentage can be lowered to 5%, that is ¼ cup salt to every 5 cups water.

The vegetables are soaked in the brine with the vinegar and other ingredients before the preserving process begins. Sometimes alum is added at the end to keep the texture of the vegetables crisp, but this shouldn't be necessary if the vegetables are in prime condition.

A typical method for brining and pickling is to cut the vegetables into suitable sizes and cover with a 5% brine for 24 hours, keeping them weighted down with a plate to cover them completely. Drain them, rinse thoroughly with cold water and cover with spiced pickling vinegar (see page 86). Remove air bubbles, then cover and process in a boiling water bath (212°). Complete the seals if necessary and let cool. Keep for at least 2 months before using.

SPICES AND HERBS

Spices add zest and flavor to pickles and relishes and also have the added advantage that they are preservatives in their own right. The best ones to use are cloves, cinnamon, pepper, allspice, mace, nutmeg and ginger. Ground turmeric is sometimes added for its golden color. Herbs are a traditional addition to many relishes and pickles, notably rue, fennel, sage, coriander and garlic and, most famous of all, dill.

Spiced Pickling Vinegar

½ oz each whole
cloves, allspice berries,
root ginger, cinnamon
sticks, whole
peppercorns
5 cups vinegar

Steep the spices in the vinegar in a large bottle, without heating, for 1–2 months, shaking occasionally. Strain the vinegar and re-bottle. Keep covered, preferably with a cork.

For a quicker method, warm the vinegar in an aluminum saucepan. Add the spices, cover and infuse over a low heat for 2 hours. Leave to cool. When cold, strain the vinegar into bottles.

VINEGAR

When making pickles and relishes, use the best quality vinegar possible, and check that it has an acetic acid content of at least 5%. Cheap vinegar is a false economy since the preserves will not keep so well. White vinegar shows off the color and texture of a pickle better than a dark one, but for most domestic purposes malt vinegar gives perfectly satisfactory results.

STORING

Pickles and relishes are best stored in glass jars. Do not use enameled containers, or any made of copper, brass or iron because these will be corroded by both the vinegar and the salt.

It is vital to keep the air out of jars of pickles and relishes since it causes discoloration, encourages molds and degrades the vinegar by facilitating the invasion of bacteria. So fill the jars and cover carefully, making sure that there are no air bubbles. Pickles must be kept well below the surface of the vinegar or brine or mixture of the two. You can put a layer of oil over the top to seal it – mustard oil is the best one to use for this since it has preservative properties.

Where the vinegar solution is fairly dilute, the pickle will not keep for all that long because of the level of acidity. You can, however, skim off any scum as it forms and still eat the contents – it is natural and harmless, but do finish the pickles as quickly as possible once this starts to happen.

Times of storage vary considerably with different pickles and relishes: some are ready quickly, whereas others may need six months or more to mature.

SERVING IDEAS

Pickles and relishes are a marvelous and colorful contribution to a salad table – when it is laid out, a buffet looks quite sumptuous with a variety of homemade pickles dotted among the dishes. They are especially delicious with cheeses, with potted meats and in sandwiches. Pickles and relishes can be mixed into cottage cheese to sharpen it up, and are also excellent with freshly boiled ham.

PICKLED MUSHROOMS (page 88)

Sweet Watermelon Rind Pickle

Whoever had the bizarre idea of pickling watermelon rind was actually rather inspired: on the face of it, it seems unlikely to be delicious, yet cooked in a spiced syrup the rind turns translucent and crunchy, and is a superb addition to a cold buffet table.

4 lb watermelon rind	2½ cups white vinegar
½ cup salt	4 teaspoons whole cloves
7½ cups cold water	2 3-inch sticks cinnamon
2 lb (5⅓ cups) sugar	

MAKES 4 lb

Peel the dark skin off the rind and scrape off any traces of the pink fruit. Cut the rind into ½-inch cubes. Dissolve the salt in 5 cups of water, add the rind cubes and steep for 6 hours.

Drain and rinse thoroughly. Put the rind into a saucepan and cover with fresh water. Simmer for 10 minutes until tender but not too soft. Drain.

Combine the sugar, vinegar and remaining 2½ cups water in an aluminum preserving kettle. Tie the cloves and cinnamon in a cheesecloth bag and add to the pan. Bring to a boil and simmer for 10 minutes. Pour the spiced vinegar over the rind cubes. Leave to stand overnight with the bag still in the mixture.

Bring to a boil again and simmer for 10 minutes until the rind is transparent. Remove the cheesecloth bag.

Transfer the rinds with a slotted spoon into hot clean jars. Pour over the hot syrup. Cover and process. Store for three weeks before using.

Pickled Mushrooms

This light and delicate method of pickling mushrooms retains their flavor and texture. They make a lovely cold side dish to go with other salads, and provide a delightful contribution to a picnic basket.

½ lb (2 cups) small button mushrooms	1¼ cups wine vinegar
	12 peppercorns
1 large onion	3 bay leaves
2 garlic cloves	sprig of rosemary
2½ cups water	sprig of thyme
2 teaspoons salt	

MAKES 1 lb

Wipe the mushrooms clean. Skin and slice the onion. Bruise the garlic.

Put the mushrooms into a saucepan with the water and salt. Bring to a boil, then remove from the heat and leave to stand for 5 minutes. Drain and dry the mushrooms with a clean dish-towel.

Put the vinegar into an aluminum preserving kettle with the spices, herbs, onion and garlic. Simmer for 15 minutes. Strain.

Place the mushrooms in a hot clean jar and pour over the hot spiced vinegar. Cover and process. Store for two to three weeks before using.

Corn Relish

When the corn crop is particularly plentiful, I love to make this relish. It is one of the most tempting both to look at and to taste. Corn relish is quite crunchy and slightly spicy, and one of the most popular all-rounders with family and friends alike.

6 ears of corn, husked	2 teaspoons flour
½ head white cabbage	2 teaspoons dry mustard
2 large onions	½ teaspoon turmeric
2 small red peppers	1 cup brown sugar
2 teaspoons salt	2½ cups vinegar

MAKES 4 lb

Put the ears of corn in a saucepan of boiling water and simmer for 3 minutes. Cool slightly then strip the corn kernels from the cobs.

Wash and mince the cabbage, onions and peppers in a food processor or meat grinder. Put into an aluminum preserving kettle with the corn.

Mix the salt, flour, mustard, turmeric and sugar together thoroughly. Gradually stir in the vinegar, blending well. Add to the vegetables and simmer for 30 minutes.

Pack the relish into hot clean jars. Cover and process.

Cucumber Relish

The translucency of cucumber, slightly sweetened and spiced, looks beautiful in this pale green relish. In my house, this disappears rapidly during the summer months – it is an indispensible part of light salad meals and is delicious with cheeses.

2 cucumbers	2⅔ cups brown sugar
3 lb green tomatoes	1 lb (2⅔ cups) white
1 green pepper	sugar
1 red pepper	2 tablespoons all-purpose
8 medium onions	flour
1 teaspoon salt	2 tablespoons curry
5 cups white vinegar	powder
	1 tablespoon dry mustard

MAKES 8 lb

Wash and finely mince all the vegetables using a food processor or meat grinder. Put into a bowl and sprinkle with 1 tablespoon salt. Cover and leave to stand overnight. Drain off the liquid.

Put the minced vegetables into an aluminum preserving kettle with the vinegar and sugar. Bring to a boil and simmer for 1 hour.

Blend the flour, curry powder and mustard with a little vinegar to make a creamy paste and stir into the pan. Simmer for a further 30 minutes.

Pack the relish into hot clean jars. Cover and process.

Malay Vegetable Pickle

Crunchy and spicy, this uniquely Indonesian pickle is full of flavor and makes a kind of salad dish in its own right, highlighting other dishes of all kinds. I was introduced to it by an Indian friend of mine and now I wonder how I ever got along without it!

1 cucumber	1⅓ cups toasted sesame
3 large carrots	seeds
½ lb cauliflower	2 teaspoons turmeric
4 green chilies	1 tablespoon chili powder
2 cups dry-roasted	¾ cup vegetable oil
peanuts	salt
6 garlic cloves	
2½ cups spiced vinegar	MAKES 5 lb
(see page 86)	
1⅓ cups light brown	
sugar	

Wash and cut the cucumber into ¼-inch slices. Wash, peel and cut the carrots into ¼-inch slices. Wash and cut the cauliflower into flowerettes. Wash and seed the chilies, then cut lengthwise. Coarsely grind the peanuts. Crush the garlic.

Bring the vinegar to a boil in an aluminum preserving kettle. Add the vegetables, one type at a time in a large sieve, and scald by dunking them into the vinegar. Shake off as much of the vinegar as possible.

In a large bowl, mix the vegetables together with the sugar, peanuts and sesame seeds. Mix the turmeric and chili powder to a paste with a little water.

Heat the oil in a pan and fry the garlic very gently for 1–2 minutes. Add the spice paste and salt to taste. Leave to cool. Stir in garlic mixture.

Pack the pickle into large, sterile jars. This pickle will keep for several months if stored in the refrigerator.

Pickled Green Walnuts

An utterly English invention, this unlikely idea has been used by the country housewife for centuries. Nothing is better in its way than a lunch of bread, cheese and pickled walnuts.

1½ lb green walnuts	6 cloves
7½ cups strong brine (see	12 peppercorns
page 85)	7½ cups spiced vinegar
4 large garlic cloves	(see page 86)
	MAKES 3 lb

Put the green walnuts into a large bowl. Pour over the brine and leave to soak for a week until they turn black. Put them into a colander and rinse thoroughly in hot water until the salt is washed off.

Prick the walnuts with a fork in order to let the spices permeate. Pack them into hot clean jars with the garlic, cloves and peppercorns among them.

Bring the spiced vinegar to a boil. Pour the hot vinegar over the walnuts. Leave to stand overnight.

Drain off the vinegar, reheat to boiling again and pour over the walnuts once more. Cover and process.

MALAY VEGETABLE PICKLE (above left)

Summer Relish

Delightfully easy to make, this is one way of converting a glut of summer vegetables so that you can enjoy them in later months. It looks gorgeous too – full of the colors of summer.

2 large carrots	⅔ cup olive oil
1 green pepper	1 tablespoon light brown
12 green beans	sugar
1 zucchini	2 tablespoons chopped
12 green olives	fresh oregano or
12 cherry tomatoes	marjoram
1 lb cauliflower	5 tablespoons water
flowerettes	salt and pepper
1¼ cups wine vinegar	
	MAKES 4 lb

Wash, peel and cut the carrots into julienne strips. Wash, seed and cut the pepper into small cubes. Trim the green beans and cut into 1-inch lengths. Wash, trim and cut the zucchini into julienne strips. Halve and pit the olives. Wash and quarter the cherry tomatoes.

Combine all the ingredients in an aluminum preserving kettle and add salt and pepper to taste. Bring to a boil and simmer, stirring constantly, for 5 minutes.

Cool and leave to marinate for 24 hours.

Bring the relish to a boil again, then pack into hot clean jars. Cover and process.

Sour Chinese Cabbage Relish

This is taken from a traditional Korean recipe, where it is known as **kimchee.** *It is a kind of non-preserved chutney, one which keeps for a relatively short time but which is so different and unusual that I love to produce it.*

1½ lb Chinese (Nappa or	1 lb (2½ cups) salt
celery) cabbage	2 tablespoons ground
4 garlic cloves	ginger
6 scallions	1 red chili
1½ quarts water	1 teaspoon sugar
	MAKES 4 lb

Wash and coarsely shred the Chinese cabbage leaves. Skin and chop the garlic. Wash, trim and finely slice the scallions. Mix the water with the salt in a bowl. Add the cabbage and leave to soak for 12 hours, turning occasionally.

Mix the ginger, garlic, scallions, chili and sugar in a large bowl. Drain the cabbage, reserving the liquid, and combine with the mixture in the bowl.

Put the cabbage mixture into a large stone crock or glass jar and cover with the salt water. Cover with a cloth and leave for about a week to ferment – it will be ready when it turns slightly sour.

Pack the relish into sterile jars. Cover and seal. Store in a cool place for not longer than three weeks.

Red Pepper Relish

A lovely, piquant, strong relish that is only needed in quite small quantities – a little goes a long way. It is absolutely superb to accompany a simple meal of an omelet, a salad and some fresh bread.

⅓ cup mustard seeds	3 lb (8 cups) white sugar
2 lb red peppers	2 quarts vinegar

MAKES 4 lb

Soak the mustard seeds in hot water for 2–3 hours. Drain. Wash and remove the seeds from the peppers. Cut the flesh into fairly fine strips.

Put all the ingredients into an aluminum preserving kettle. Bring slowly to a boil, stirring until the sugar has dissolved. Boil rapidly for 15–20 minutes, stirring frequently, until the liquid begins to thicken.

Pack the relish into hot clean jars. Cover and process.

Fresh Coriander Relish

A typically Indian relish, this has a short storage life but is so delicious that I cannot resist making it when coriander is plentiful. The coconut milk provides a lovely smoothness, and the balance of the garlic and spices with the coriander makes a very special condiment for a spicy eastern meal.

1 tablespoon shredded dried coconut	3 small green chilies
	juice of 2 limes
1¼ cups boiling water	½ teaspoon salt
2 bunches fresh coriander	1 teaspoon brown sugar
2 garlic cloves	1 teaspoon ground cumin
½-inch piece fresh ginger root	

MAKES 2 lb

Allow the coconut to steep in the boiling water for 30 minutes. Wash and chop the coriander. Crush the garlic. Peel and grate the ginger. Wash and chop the chilies. Blend the coconut mixture in a food processor or blender, then strain through a sieve.

Combine remaining ingredients with the coconut milk and blend in a food processor, adding a very little water if necessary to obtain a smooth paste.

Pack the relish into sterile jars. Cover and seal. Store in the refrigerator for up to three weeks.

Tomato Relish

A lovely sharp, fresh relish with a light spiciness to it. With its contrasting textures of tomatoes, cucumber and red pepper, this mixture is delicious with cold meats.

3 lb tomatoes	1 tablespoon dry mustard
1 lb cucumber	½ teaspoon ground
2 oz salt	allspice
2 garlic cloves	½ teaspoon mustard
1 large red pepper	seeds
2 cups white vinegar	
	MAKES ABOUT 3 lb

Skin and slice the tomatoes. Peel, seed and roughly chop the cucumber. Layer the tomatoes and cucumber in a bowl, sprinkling each layer with salt. Cover and leave to stand overnight.

Strain off the liquid and rinse well and place in a large saucepan. Skin and finely chop the garlic. Wash, seed and roughly chop the pepper and add these to the pan. Blend the vinegar with the dry ingredients, stir into the pan and bring slowly to the boil. Simmer gently for about 1 hour, stirring occasionally, until the mixture is soft. Spoon the relish into warm, clean jars and cover. Seal immediately. Store for 3–4 months before use.

Sweet-Sour Apricots

I love fresh apricots – one of the most delicate and beautiful of our summer fruits, I always think. Preserved in this way, with a tang and spiciness added to their natural fruitiness, they also look glorious nestling in their glistening syrup.

1⅛ cups (12 fl oz) wine	1 lb apricots
vinegar	1 small cinnamon stick
9 oz granulated sugar	

Pour the vinegar into a saucepan, add the sugar and heat gently, stirring, until the sugar has dissolved, then bring to the boil. Peel the apricots. Put the apricots into a warm, clean jar, packing as lightly as possible, add the cinnamon stick and slowly pour in the hot vinegar syrup. Cover immediately with an airtight and vinegar-proof top.

Note: These pickled apricots are best left for a month before using. Serve with pork, ham or chicken.

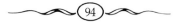

Index